FAITH TO LIVE BY

A PRACTICAL GUIDE
TO THE LIFE OF FAITH

PAUL BARKER

EVERY NATION PRODUCTIONS
BRENTWOOD, TENNESSEE

Published by Every Nation Productions
P.O. Box 1787 Brentwood, TN 37024-1787 USA

ISBN 978-0-9752848-0-3

*This book is dedicated to my wife Aleta.
Her love and encouragement have been my constant
inspiration for thirty-three amazing years.*

CONTENTS

ACKNOWLEDGMENTS

The great thing about writing this book is it gives me the opportunity to publicly thank many of the people who have been influential in shaping my life and thought.

To my wife Aleta, thank you for always being my number one fan—what a mess I would be without you. Thank you for always seeking God's kingdom first throughout our entire marriage.

To my four children and their spouses, Samuel and Kerren, Joseph and Leigh, Katie and Ernie, and Jessica and Barry, thank you for making life so fun, full, and rich.

To my Dad and Mom, thank you for the many sacrifices you made to give me a foundation of faith.

To Gregg Tipton, thank you for the continual inspiration of passion for the Great Commission that you provide. This book would not have happened if it wasn't for the faith you live by.

To Steve Murrell, thank you for being an example of what a godly leader should be.

To Rice Broocks, thank you for demonstrating a living testimony of what the life of faith should look like.

To Joey Bonifacio, Manny Carlos, and all the leaders of the Victory Church in the Philippines, thank you for giving me a place to grow, learn, and teach.

To Bob Weiner, thank you for giving me a start in ministry and believing in me when that was a very risky proposition.

To David Houston, thank you for being a friend and pastor for more than thirty years.

To Michael Shepard, thank you for being my friend and constant encourager. If only I could be like you when I grow up.

To Steve Ottolini and Mike Hayden, thank you for a decade of life and ministry together. You shaped my life in so many important ways.

To Joe & Pat Clendenny, thank you for your great passion to support God's work all over the world. What a great reward awaits you!

To our ministry partners, thank you for giving of yourself so that we can fulfill God's calling. We could not do it without you.

To everyone who worked on this book with me: thank you, Varsha Daswani, for proofing my writing several times until I could get it right. Thank you, Edwin Navarro, for walking me through the printing process. Thank you, Samuel Barker, for all the graphic designs in the book.

FOREWORD

Right now, while writing this foreword, I am in a room in the Every Nation building in Manila with fifteen Filipinos and one white guy, discussing an upcoming sermon series that will be preached at ninety-one weekend worship services in sixteen Victory Manila congregations. Eventually, these sermons will spread beyond Metro Manila to all over Asia and other parts of the world where Filipino missionaries serve as cross-cultural church planters.

We are in the middle of an interesting theological discussion about the difference between propitiation and expiation, with English, Filipino, and Greek words being thrown around. The conversation goes from intense to hilarious, from theological issues to Manny Pacquiao's upcoming fight. At some point when the conversation meanders into pure Filipino, the white guy clears his throat, and the conversation immediately bounces back to English. I love this team, and I love my job!

Over the years, I have been in hundreds of these sermon preparation meetings, discussing, debating, laughing, and arguing as we prepare sermons together for our Victory Manila congregations. Lately, these meetings have been better than ever. The theological, historical, hermeneutical discussion points are deeper and more focused. We seem to accomplish more in less time. Our sermon prep meetings have always been good, but I think they have recently gone from good to great.

There are many reasons for the progress, including the maturity of those in the room, the unity of the team, and the meetings before the meetings that help keep the discussions focused on the one big point.

Another reason our Victory Manila sermon prep meetings are better than ever is the white guy in the room— Paul Barker. Paul's passion for in-depth Bible study, Christ-centered preaching, accurate Bible interpretation, and historical context has really upgraded our team's perspective.

A couple of years ago, after several ministry trips to help equip Filipino leaders, Paul was asked by the Victory Manila leadership team to invest more time in the Philippines. He now splits his time between Manila and Nashville.

I have worked with Paul in ministry since the early eighties. And I have always known him to be not only a man who seriously studies and accurately preaches God's Word, but also one who has contagious faith. That combination of serious scholarship and childlike faith makes for a valuable perspective on the life of faith.

Faith is one of the most important topics we will ever study. Without it, we cannot please God. Faith is also one of the most misunderstood topics. Like you, I have listened to countless sermons on faith and read scores of books on faith. Some of these sermons and books have been biblical and helpful, others not so much.

I think you will find Paul's writings on faith to be both biblical and helpful.

I am glad Paul finally put his faith teachings into writing, and I am glad you are reading them. I trust this book will not only stretch your faith, but will inspire you to a deeper, more accurate study of God's Word.

Steve Murrell
President, Every Nation Churches and Ministries

PREFACE

What is Different about this Series?

This is the first of a two-part series on *faith*. The questions we must first answer are, "Why do we need more books on faith? What is different about this series?"

First, it is comprehensive. I have attempted to examine the essential issues in as thorough a manner as possible. No doubt I have missed some topics, and overemphasized or underemphasized others. But I have done my best to make this series as complete as possible.

Second, it is sequential. I have attempted to cover all the related topics in the order that will best help you understand and grow in your faith.

Third, it is rooted in history. I am a fervent student of Church history, and I am passionate that we draw from the collective resources of 2,000 years of men and women who walked with God and learned from Him. I believe that any topic as vast as faith should be understood in light of what the Church has said about it throughout Her long history.

Fourth, it is a composite of different perspectives. My views on faith have been shaped by a diversity of ministries. I don't necessarily agree with everything each one of them says, but I have learned something about faith from all of them. One piece of a 1000-piece jigsaw puzzle can never represent the whole picture; even a section of the puzzle can't. But when you put all the pieces together, then you see the picture clearly.

I recently listened to two different podcasts on the same day from ministers on opposite ends of the theological spectrum.

Both said disparaging things about the other person's beliefs. But both greatly helped me understand the topic of faith. I wondered if either of the ministers had engaged the other in a serious dialogue to understand his position better. I couldn't help thinking that if they had, they would have discovered that God had given each of them a piece of the puzzle, and the picture would never be complete until they (and we) start putting the sections together.

Fifth, it is an interactive study for individual or small group ministry. Each chapter has a verse to memorize, questions to discuss (designed especially for small groups), and action points. There is also a wealth of varied material in the several appendices.

My objective in writing this series was to create a definitive workbook that would provide you with everything you need to develop a dynamic life of faith. May God bless you as you read and study His Word. As Charles Spurgeon said:

> "Faith is the mightiest of the mighty. It is the monarch of the realms of the mind. There is no being superior to its strength, no creature that will not bow to its divine prowess. The lack of faith makes a person despicable; it shrivels him up so small that he might live in a nutshell. Give him faith, and he is a leviathan that can dive into the depths of the sea, a giant who takes nations and crumbles them in his hand, vanquishing hosts with his sword and gathering up all the crowns as his own. There is nothing like faith. Faith makes you almost as omnipotent as God, by borrowed power of its divinity. Give us faith and we can do all things." [1]

---

[1] Charles H. Spurgeon, The Triumph of Faith in a Believer's Life (Lynnwood, WA: Emerald Books, 1994), 128.

CHAPTER 1

The Life of Faith:
Building Foundations that will Last

Faith did not come easy for me. I do not know why it took me so long to understand what I now see are very simple concepts, but it did. And if it weren't for God's mercy and grace, I would still be confused.

I don't think I am alone. I am not sure of all the reasons, but faith seems to be a challenging concept to comprehend for many people. Maybe because it goes against our natural mind, or maybe because the enemy fights so hard to keep it from us—but for whatever reasons, it is a difficult concept for many of us to grasp.

In this chapter, I want to share with you my journey of faith. Hopefully it will encourage you, and it may even shed light on your own journey. It will certainly give you a context for everything else I say in this book.

My Journey of Faith

I was born and raised in metro St. Louis, Missouri, the home of the St. Louis Cardinals, Ted Drewes Frozen Custard, and Imo's pizza—all St. Louis institutions. My parents were devout Roman Catholics. They worked hard to make sure I received a good Catholic education. I am very grateful for the foundation it laid in my life. Even when I tried desperately to escape from God during my agnostic college years, I knew deep within that there was a God. I knew I could never escape from Him, no matter how hard I tried. C.S. Lewis once said in reference to his conversion:

> "You must picture me alone in that room in Magdelen College, night after night, feeling the steady, unrelenting approach of Him whom I so earnestly desired not to meet."[1]

I felt a lot like that.

I went to university at Southeast Missouri State in Cape Girardeau. My hobby was attending dorm Bible studies and disrupting them with pseudo-intellectual questions (heavy emphasis on the word "pseudo"). I usually left triumphant because, unfortunately, I knew my stuff better than most of the Christians did.

But there was one guy on my dorm floor who refused to argue with me. His name was Mike and he was from a small farming community about an hour north of the university. He was a sincere and unpretentious fellow, and I don't think he felt qualified to engage me at an intellectual level. Whenever I would present my latest argument (usually something I learned that day in Psychology or Biology class), he would listen patiently to my rant. When I finished, he would look me in the eyes and say, "I don't know how to answer your questions. But I do know that Jesus loves you, and He wants to change your life."

How I hated when he said that! I could deal with intellectual rebuttals—I welcomed them—but I had no answer to that response.

---

[1]   C. S. Lewis, Surprised by Joy: The Shape of My Early Life *(1955), Chapter XIV.*

Eventually, as my personal life deteriorated, God's love broke through my hardened exterior and I surrendered my life to Him. It was Sunday, July 11, 1976.

Soon after my conversion, I became aware that God was calling me to serve Him in vocational ministry. Three years later, I graduated from university and married my wife, the former Aleta Mueller. Two days after our honeymoon, we started our life in ministry together.

Within a few months we received a call from a pastor in Knoxville, Tennessee who led a small campus church at the University of Tennessee. He was in need of an associate and wanted us to work with him. So on Thursday, October 25, 1979, we packed everything we owned in our 1974 Audi Fox and drove to Knoxville. Fifteen months later, the pastor left to start a new campus church in Arizona. He left me in charge. I was twenty-four years old and clueless.

I did the best I could leading that small church, but it was an uphill climb. I did not really know what I was doing, so I tried every new thing that came my way. But month after month, our membership declined. I was losing the battle, and I was not even sure why.

Every two months, I attended meetings with the other leaders in the organization of campus churches I belonged to, and each time I heard testimonies of successful activities that had worked in other locations. And so every two months, I instituted a new program. But nothing ever worked out very well.

But in the fall of 1981 while attending one of these meetings, I heard what I was sure must be the key to my success. A pastor told about conducting a full month of outreach meetings at his campus. Many were saved, he testified, and great things had happened. Certainly this was the answer to my dilemma.

So in the month of November, I staged a full month of outreach activities. We had special speakers, music groups, evangelistic films, street preaching, and everything else you could imagine. But after one month of daily meetings, I had very little to show for my labor. The church members were tired and disgruntled. The budget was in disarray. And there were no salvations. (Two people did raise their hands at the end of one meeting, but as soon as we dismissed the service they ran from the building as fast as they could. I did not feel that it was right to count them among the converted.)

That was it for me. I had done everything I knew and nothing had worked. I seriously considered resigning from the ministry. Maybe I could drive a truck or sell shoes or do something that was actually helping someone. I was sure that what I was doing in ministry was not helping anyone.

I did not know it at the time, but I later realized that God was orchestrating the details of my life to get my attention. My circumstances had put me in a listening frame of mind. I was desperate and open to anything God had to say. Solomon said, *One who is full loathes honey from the comb, but to the hungry even what is bitter tastes sweet* (Proverbs 27:7). I was very hungry and ready for anything God had for me.

About this time, someone gave me a set of audio tapes by a well-known preacher. I had heard this man speak before, and frankly, I was not impressed. He was a businessman who had built a successful faith teaching ministry. His message was simple and straightforward, but his delivery style was one of a kind. I had a university degree in English, and he did things to the English language that I don't think had ever been done before. I found it difficult to listen to him, and even harder to believe God was speaking to me through him.

But though his grammar was questionable, his faith was not. I listened to these tapes continuously for weeks. Gradually, I noticed a change taking place. Not on the outside—people were still staying away from our church in crowds—but on the inside. Something was changing in me. I was beginning to think differently. A new image was growing on the inside. I started to see that I could experience success and fruitfulness because of God's Word and His promises.

In the first week of January 1982, I read the following verse from Luke's Gospel:

> When he had finished speaking, he said to Simon, "Put out into deep water, and let down the nets for a catch." Simon answered, "Master, we've worked hard all night and haven't caught anything. But because you say so, I will let down the nets."
>
> LUKE 5:4,5

Like the disciples, I had toiled hard at fishing, and like them, I had caught nothing. But Jesus was asking me to put my nets out again. So I scheduled another outreach meeting. This time I was not as ambitious as before (three days instead of a month), and this time I was acting on His Word—not on someone else's good idea. I saturated the event with prayer and strong faith confessions, and waited expectantly to see what God would do.

When the meetings were over, seventy-five students had given their lives to Christ. I know that is not a large amount when compared with big campaigns, but considering my situation, it was a landslide! Through this experience I began to understand many of the essential biblical concepts of how faith works. And the truth I learned became part of the foundations I would continue to build my life upon.

Having the right foundations is crucial to a successful Christian life. Before we begin an examination of what faith is and how it works, let's look at some principles related to foundations.

Foundations

The dictionary defines a foundation as "the basis on which a thing stands or is supported. A foundation bears the weight of what is built upon it." Foundations are the core principles our lives are built upon. The Bible has a lot to say about foundations and their importance in our lives.

If we do not get our foundations right at the beginning, the repair costs can be very high at the end.

It took nearly 200 years to construct the 190-foot freestanding bell tower next to the cathedral in Pisa, Italy. But because of a weak foundation, the tower began leaning even before construction finished in 1372. By 1988, the tower was leaning fifteen feet off-center. They closed it to tourists for fear that it would topple. However, after ten years and $27,000,000 in repairs, workers finally succeeded in anchoring the tower with a permanent 13.5-foot lean. (No tourist would pay to see the "Straight Tower of Pisa"!)

Anything built on faulty foundations will collapse in time. If we do not build a proper foundation of faith, we will look like the Leaning Tower of Pisa. And it will take a huge investment and a lot of time to set things right. That is why the Psalmist said:

> "When the foundations are being destroyed, what can the righteous do?"
>
> PSALM 11:3

The higher we want our lives to go, the deeper we have to build our foundations.

The main building on the campus of Philippine Christian College in Cabanatuan City, Philippines, was built in 1964 with three stories. The foundation the builders laid was sufficient for a building of that size. But a few years later the school added three additional stories without making any changes to the foundation. In 1990, a 7.8 earthquake hit the region, killing 1,600 people. All of the three-story buildings in Cabanatuan City were untouched. The only building to collapse was the six-story school building, and over 100 students and staff members died. The earthquake proved that the foundation was strong enough for three floors, but inadequate for six.

What dreams and aspirations do you have for your life? The larger the dream, the deeper the foundations must be.

Coach Mike Krzyzewski of the Duke University Blue Devils is widely recognized as one of the most successful college basketball coaches in the history of the NCAA. In twenty-eight years at Duke, he has won three NCAA Championships, ten ACC Championships, and twelve National Coach of the Year honors. And maybe the most impressive statistic of all is that only two of his athletes have failed to graduate. Coach K said recently about his accomplishments, "It has been my goal to give Duke a program that will last." Enduring programs require deep foundations, and so do enduring lives.

Building strong foundations is hard work.

I learned this the hard way several years ago when I decided that the deck in our backyard had to go. It was old, small, and beginning to rot. I am not very handy when it comes to home projects, so I hired a friend of mine who taught Industrial Education at one of the local high schools. His job was to design and oversee the project, and mine was to provide the labor, with the help of my two teenage sons. The first task he assigned us was to destroy the old deck. That was demanding work because it was the middle of the summer and the temperature was near 100 °F every day. But there is something deeply satisfying about swinging a sledge hammer and destroying stuff, so I almost enjoyed it. However, I was not prepared for what was to come.

The next task was to dig foundations for the new structure. Because my plans called for a much larger deck than before (it would seat around thirty-five people), I had to dig four deep holes to support it. That was excruciatingly painful. (I kept thinking about that fellow in Luke 16 who was too ashamed to beg and too weak to dig. I could identify with him completely.)

After the holes were finally dug, we made an appointment with the city building inspector. If the holes met the proper standards, he would issue me a permit and I could proceed with the project. If not, I would have to try again until I got it right. I prayed for a merciful inspector, but instead I got "Legalistic Larry." He measured the holes with care and then delivered the bad news: "Unacceptable." I would have to keep digging.

I did get the holes right the second time. We poured the foundations and finally started the interesting work of constructing the deck. But I learned a valuable lesson in the process: laying foundations is hard work. That is why many people start the work of laying strong faith foundations, but do not finish. The work is too demanding, and the pressure is too great. In the end, they take the path of least resistance.

The challenges of life reveal how strong our foundations are.

> When the whirlwind passes, the wicked is no more, but the righteous has an everlasting foundation.
> Proverbs 10:25 (NASB)

Storms happen to everyone, and some get swept away by them. But those with a strong foundation are unmoved. Jesus never promised us storm-free lives. Storms will come; we cannot avoid them. However, we can storm-proof our lives by building them upon a solid foundation of obedience to God's Word.

> "Therefore everyone who hears these words of mine and puts them into practice is like a wise man who built his house on the rock. The rain came down, the streams rose, and the winds blew and beat against that house; yet it did not fall, because it had its foundation on the rock. But everyone who hears these words of mine and does not put them into practice is like a foolish man who built his house on sand. The rain came down, the streams rose, and the winds blew and beat against that house, and it fell with a great crash."
> Matthew 7:24-27

Paul confirmed these words of Jesus when he told the Corinthians . . . *the fire will test the quality of each person's work* (1 Corinthians 3:13).

At 6:34 PM local time on Sunday, August 8, 1993, an 8.1 earthquake shook the island of Guam. It lasted for a full minute. Buildings swayed, vehicles moved, and the ground opened up in places. The quake damaged structures and lifelines throughout the island. However, not a single building collapsed, and injuries were generally minor. Why was there such minimal damage? Because nearly all the buildings in Guam were built with a solid foundation of reinforced concrete. Construction in Guam is governed by the Uniform Building Code, the same standard used in most seismically active regions of North America. The officials in Guam knew an earthquake was coming, they just did not know when it would come or how big it would be. But they were prepared with stringent building codes to endure earthquakes of any size.

No one likes strict building codes during the building phase. They are expensive and time-consuming. But everyone likes strict building codes when their buildings are still standing after a severe earthquake. In the same way, we generally do not like building our personal lives according to strict codes—especially when there are so many shortcuts available and so many people who seem to be taking them. But when the earthquakes and the storms of life sweep by with no damage, we are glad we built our lives upon the solid foundation of faith in God!

And we can be sure that difficult days are coming. As Paul told Timothy . . .

> But mark this: There will be terrible times in the last days.
>
> 2 TIMOTHY 3:1

Timothy must have thought that difficult times had already begun! Paul had left him with the "wild beasts and false teachers" in Ephesus,[2] and he was obviously struggling under the pressure. Timothy was not always a confident man (1 Corinthians 16:10). He seemed to have struggled with fear and intimidation (2 Timothy 1:7,8). Paul regularly urged him to be strong (2 Timothy 2:1,3). But Timothy had strong foundations, and Paul knew it.

> But as for you, continue in what you have learned and have become convinced of, because you know those from whom you learned it, and how from infancy you have known the Holy Scriptures, which are able to make you wise for salvation through faith in Christ Jesus.
>
> 2 TIMOTHY 3:14,15

Strong foundations were first laid in Timothy's life by his mother and grandmother. Jewish boys began their formal study of the Scriptures at age five.[3] Timothy's mother and grandmother had no doubt begun teaching him at an even earlier age because the Greek word Paul used, *brephos*, refers to a newborn child or an infant.[4]

---

[2] *1 Corinthians 15:32, 1 Timothy 1:3.*
[3] *Don Closson,* Hermeneutics, *www.probe.org.*
[4] *It can also refer to an unborn child still in the womb. It is possible that Lois and Eunice started speaking the Word to Timothy before he was even born.*

Paul then reinforced those foundations and built upon them when he began to disciple Timothy.

> Now you followed my teaching, conduct, purpose, faith, patience, love, perseverance . . .
>
> 2 TIMOTHY 3:10 (NASB)

Conclusion

Timothy survived and even conquered in difficult times because of the strong foundations in his life. The author of Hebrews tells us that faith towards God is one of the essential qualities necessary to a strong foundation.

> Therefore let us move beyond the elementary teachings about Christ and be taken forward to maturity, not laying again the foundation of repentance from acts that lead to death, and of faith in God . . .
>
> HEBREWS 6:1

One of the primary goals of this series is to help you build strong foundations of faith.

In this chapter, we have examined the importance of laying strong foundations of faith in our lives. But exactly why is faith so important? We will examine that question in the next chapters.

APPLICATION

Discuss

1. What are the main challenges you have with the message of faith? Why? What can you do to face these challenges and begin to overcome them?

_____

_____

_____

2. How strong is the foundation of faith in your life? Has there ever been a time in your life when it was stronger? If so, what has changed, and what can you do to get back to the place where you were?

_____

_____

_____

3. How big are your dreams, and is your current foundation of faith strong enough to sustain them? If not, what areas need the most work, and what should you do about them?

_____

_____

_____

4. When was the last time you received bad news? How did you respond? What did God show you about the foundations of your faith through that response? What is the key to a proper response the next time bad news comes?

_____

_____

_____

Act

Do a personal inventory of your foundations. Take thirty minutes and ask the Holy Spirit to reveal to you what area of your foundations needs the most work. Ask Him for a plan to strengthen your foundations.

Memorize

"When the foundations are being destroyed, what can the righteous do?"

PSALM 11:3

CHAPTER 2

Why do We Need Faith?
Part 1

One of the first words my children learned to say when they were growing up was "why." There were periods during their early development when it seemed like that was the most important word in their vocabulary.

"Why is ice slippery?"

"Why don't cats cry?"

"Why is broccoli green?"

Answering all the "why" questions was often exasperating. But it helped me greatly when I finally realized that my children were only responding to the desire that God had put in them to understand and know the reasons and causes behind the things around them. God has put this same desire to understand and know "why" in all our hearts. It is a part of the image of God in man—what theologians call the *Imago Dei*.[1]

So it seems like a good idea to start this book on the life of faith by asking and answering the all-important "why" questions: Why do I need faith? Why is faith so important?

In this chapter and the next, we will look at eight reasons we need faith.

---

[1] Imago Dei *is Latin for "The Image of God."*

We need faith to please God.

When I fell in love with my wife many years ago, I determined to find out all the things that pleased her. As I discovered them, I set about making it my life's ambition to practice them with all my heart. I haven't always succeeded in our thirty-three years together, but I am still pursuing that course.

In the same way, when a man loves God, he should make it his ambition to find out all the things that please Him. When he discovers those things, he should make it his life's ambition to practice them with all his heart. The New Testament concurs with this sentiment, and states several things about pleasing God:

- Ephesians 5:10 exhorts us to *find out what pleases the Lord.*
- Second Corinthians 5:9 exhorts us to *make it our goal to please him.*
- First Thessalonians 2:4 exhorts us not to try to *please people but God, who tests our hearts.*
- Colossians 1:10 exhorts us to so live that we may *please him in every way.*

But of all the things it tells us about pleasing the Lord, the one thing that stands out the most is how we please Him.

And without faith it is impossible to please God, because anyone who comes to him must believe that he exists and that he rewards those who earnestly seek him.

HEBREWS 11:6

Marvin Vincent, in his book, *Word Studies of the Epistles*, explains that the word "please" is used in the aorist tense in this verse. The aorist tense provides an emphasis that is lost in the English translations. The emphasis is that you cannot please God *at all or in any way* without faith. Vincent also says that this word is stated in such a way as to be a universal proposition without reference to any particular time frame. In other words, faith has always been the only way to please God in ages past, and it will always be the only way to please God in the ages to come.[2]

There are many benefits to a life of faith: health, prosperity, peace, victory over sin, etc., and we will discuss each of these as we progress. However, the one benefit that seems to be talked about the least is in fact the most important: faith is how we please God. Much of the discussion about faith centers on our individual needs and what is in it for us. That is the human side of faith, and it certainly is valid. But the primary focus of faith should be on God and what it means to Him. This should be the central focus of our lives. As Martin Luther said in his *Commentary on the Book of Galatians*:

> "In my heart reigns this one article, faith in my dear Lord Christ, the beginning, middle, and end of whatever spiritual and divine thoughts I may have, whether by day or by night."

If pleasing God is our goal and life's ambition, then it is futile to do things we think please Him but in reality do not.

---

[2] Vincent's Word Studies, *Volume 4, The Epistles.*

When I was eleven, I gave my dad a book for his birthday, and it was called *The True Story of Bonnie and Clyde*. There was one problem, however: he did not want the book—I did. To this day, I can still remember the look on his face when I gave it to him. He obviously had no interest in the book and was not especially pleased with my present. He was polite and appreciative, but he knew I had bought it for him because I wanted to read it myself. I had not taken the time to discover what would please him. I simply did what I thought would please him—primarily because I knew it would please me.

Fortunately, God is very clear about what pleases Him; there is no mystery. Faith is what pleases God. Bible reading, prayer, giving, evangelism—these are all important things, but they do not please God, at least not without faith. Therefore, since it is *impossible* to please God without faith, we should make the pursuit of faith our number one goal.

The author of Hebrews uses this word "impossible" in two other places. In 6:18 he tells us *it is impossible for God to lie*. In 10:4 he tells us *it is impossible for the blood of bulls to take away sins*. The conclusion we can derive from his other uses of the word "impossible" is that it is just as likely to please God without faith as it is *for the blood of bulls to take away sins* or *for God to lie*. In other words, it is *not* going to happen.

The author uses another form of the word "please" later in the text:

> But My righteous one shall live by faith; and if he shrinks back, My soul has no pleasure in him. But we are not of those who shrink back to destruction, but of those who have faith to the preserving of the soul.
> HEBREWS 10:38,39 (NASB)

God has no pleasure in those who shrink from faith into fear or cowardice. Adam Clarke said in his commentary on this passage:

> "The word *hupostellein* [the Greek word translated 'shrinks back'] signifies, not only to draw back, but to slink away and hide through fear. As cowards are hated by all men, so those that slink away from Christ and His cause, for fear of persecution or secular loss, in them God cannot delight."[3]

There are serious consequences to not living by faith and this is a sobering reality. The writer of Hebrews states clearly that if we will not live by faith, the only other option is to shrink back—not just to some neutral state—but to destruction. The Greek word translated "destruction" here is *apoleia*, which means ruin or loss, either physically, spiritually, or eternally. This same word is also used in other sobering passages in the New Testament.

> "Enter through the narrow gate. For wide is the gate and broad is the road that leads to destruction [*apoleia*], and many enter through it."
>
> MATTHEW 7:13

> Those who want to get rich fall into temptation and a trap and into many foolish and harmful desires that plunge people into ruin and destruction [*apoleia*].
>
> 1 TIMOTHY 6:9

---

[3] Adam Clarke Commentary *on Hebrews 10:38.*

> He writes the same way in all his letters, speaking in them of these matters. His letters contain some things that are hard to understand, which ignorant and unstable people distort, as they do the other Scriptures, to their own destruction [*apoleia*].
>
> 2 PETER 3:16

Clearly, destruction is not a very appealing option. Therefore, just as we are determined to please God with our faith, we should be determined not to displease Him through our unbelief.

We need faith to live by.

Faith is not something we do occasionally. It is how we live every moment of every day. Every activity of life, from the most mundane to the most sublime, should be done by faith. This is the sentiment reflected in one of the most quoted Old Testament verses by the apostolic writers:

> "The righteous will live by faith."
>
> ROMANS 1:17

I once heard someone say that many believers have a "spare tire faith." The spare tire is that thing you hope you never have to use—and, in case of emergency, you hope you remember how to use it.

I am not mechanically inclined. I know very little about cars and how they work, but I do know how to change a flat tire. At least I thought I did. A few years ago, I had a tire blowout on the interstate. I was forced to the side of the road and had to change my tire while hundreds of cars flew by me at great speeds. I suppose I must have choked under the pressure because after changing the tire, I found that the car would not move. Exasperated, I called a friend to help me. When he arrived, he gave me the embarrassing news that I had put the tire on backwards.

Faith in the New Testament is not a spare tire. We don't just use it during emergencies. The Scriptures exhort us to *live by faith*—not to occasionally dabble in faith. That means that we do everything by faith. Not just spiritual things like prayer and Bible reading—but everything! We wake up by faith, we brush our teeth by faith, we drive to work by faith, we get parking spaces by faith. We do everything by faith!

For example, my son used to play basketball. Several years ago as a high school freshman, he struggled with his free throw shooting. His percentage was around 55%—not bad for a freshman—but he knew he could do better. During the middle of his season, I commented after a game that his free throw shooting had improved noticeably in his last six games. When we calculated his percentage during those games it was almost 85%. He said, "Dad, before I shoot, I quote the Bible verse: 'I am more than a conqueror through Christ who makes me strong.'"

I said, "Son, I don't think that is one verse, but it is actually two verses stuck together."

He responded, "I don't care, Dad, it's working."

The moral of the story is: faith works in the everyday experiences of life.

Often the message of faith is associated exclusively with healing and prosperity. Healing and prosperity are important (especially when you are sick and broke!) and faith is required for both, but faith is for much more than just healing and prosperity. It is for every area of life.

To understand healing and prosperity, let's look at it as part of the preseason. In the preseason, a team prepares for the regular season, and as part of this preparation, they play preseason games. These games are real contests played against real opponents. But the main purpose of the contest is to prepare the athletes for the more difficult upcoming games and to help them discover their weaknesses and strengths. Then when the regular season begins, they will be more effective.

I don't want to minimize the importance of healing and prosperity because a significant part of the second book in this series is dedicated to these two topics. But learning how to believe God in these areas can help train us on how faith works. We can then use these lessons to live by faith in every area of life.

Reading through the list of men and women of faith in Hebrews 11, you will see that faith for them was a lot more than just healing and prosperity—they did everything by faith. Here is a partial list of the things they did by faith and the things we should do by faith:

By faith we understand. (v. 3)
By faith we give. (v. 4)
By faith we prepare. (v. 7)
By faith we obey. (v. 8)
By faith we receive. (v. 11)
By faith we sacrifice. (v. 17)
By faith we refuse. (v. 24)
By faith we leave. (v. 27)
By faith we conquer. (v. 33)
By faith we obtain. (v. 33)

This is also reflected in Paul's statement: … *we walk by faith, not by sight* (2 Corinthians 5:7 NASB). The original Greek word translated "walk" in this verse is *peripateo*. It is a word that referred to both the physical act of walking and to a person's general conduct or behavior. When Paul said, "We walk by faith and not by sight," he meant that we should conduct our lives by the information received from the Word of God and not from our five physical senses. This does not mean we ignore the physical world, but that we reference a higher source of information for decisions. We conduct every aspect of our lives by faith.

What does it mean to live by faith? It means that we are continually aware of the promises of God and how they affect our current situation.

We need faith to do God's work.

The Apostle John records a time when the crowds followed Jesus to Capernaum. They asked Him,

> "What must we do to do the works God requires?"
> Jesus answered, "The work of God is this: to believe
> in the one he has sent."
>
> JOHN 6:28,29

What is the work God requires? What is the mandate He has given us? To *go and make disciples of all nations* (Matthew 28:19). We need to understand that Jesus did not say, "Go and make disciples *in* all nations," but He said, "Go and make disciples *of* all nations." This is the Great Commission, and in order to accomplish it, we must first make disciples in a nation, and then proceed to make the whole nation a disciple. Or, to say it another way, evangelism and discipleship is followed by the transformation of society. Therefore, God's work includes world evangelism *and* world transformation. These are not just difficult tasks—they are impossible. But "*what is impossible with man is possible with God*" (Luke 18:27). The Great Commission is going to take faith.

When my children were young, they used to watch a cartoon called *Pinky and the Brain*. The show featured the antics of two mice, a smart one (the Brain) and a dumb one (Pinky). Every episode began the same way. Pinky would ask the Brain, "Gee, Brain, what do you want to do tonight?" And the Brain would always reply, "The same thing we do every night, Pinky— try to take over the world." This is the Great Commission in cartoon version. Our job description is to try to take over the world every day—one disciple at a time. This mandate can only be accomplished through pursuing a life of faith.

Another reason we need faith to do God's work is because every time we increase our effectiveness in accomplishing the Great Commission, we should anticipate a new attack from our enemy. As someone once said, "For every new level, there is a new devil." The resistance increases as we set about to engage the enemy and take ground for the kingdom of God. There are many well-meaning believers that have set out on this path and ended up shipwrecked.

> Timothy, my son, I am giving you this command in keeping with the prophecies once made about you, so that by recalling them you may fight the battle well, holding on to faith and a good conscience, which some have rejected and so have suffered shipwreck with regard to the faith.
>
> 1 TIMOTHY 1:18,19

What did these shipwrecked believers reject? They rejected the good fight of faith. They rejected the need to hold on to faith. They rejected a good conscience. As a result, the enemy overwhelmed them and they ended up shipwrecked.

There is not much demonic pressure on people who are only looking to do the "Minimum Daily Requirement" of the Christian life. Those who are just looking to get by and not cause too much difficulty for the enemy are rarely troubled by intense demonic pressure. But the minute they decide to do something for God, they can anticipate that the enemy will attack them like a roaring lion.

I am sure there must be a special battalion of demons assigned to Christians who are determined to do their part in fulfilling the Great Commission. Because of this, our faith must be strong when we set about to do God's work, and we must continue to increase it or we may end up shipwrecked.

We can only do God's work with God's power. And faith allows us to access the power God has made available to us. Charles Spurgeon said:

> "Many grand deeds have also been born of faith, for faith works wonders. Faith in its natural form is an all-prevailing force."[4]

When asked to explain where the power came from to heal a man crippled from his birth who was now walking and jumping and praising God, Peter said:

---

[4] *Charles H. Spurgeon,* The Triumph of Faith in a Believer's Life *(Lynnwood, WA: Emerald Books, 1994), 36.*

"By faith in the name of Jesus, this man whom you see and know was made strong. It is Jesus' name and the faith that comes through him that has given this complete healing to him, as you can all see."

ACTS 3:16

How much power is available to us by faith? Paul tells us in Ephesians 1:19 when he talks about:

. . . his *incomparably great power* for us who believe. (NIV)

. . . the *exceeding greatness of His power* toward us who believe. (NKJV)

. . . the *surpassing greatness of His power* toward us who believe. (NASB)

. . . the *incredible greatness of God's power* for us who believe him. (NLT)

. . . the *immeasurable greatness of his power* in us who believe. (RSV)

. . . the *unlimited greatness of his power* . . . (God's Word)

This power, Paul said, is *according to the working of His mighty power which He worked in Christ when He raised Him from the dead* . . . (Ephesians 1:19,20 NASB). The phrase "according to" is a preposition that means "as determined by."

Think of it as a credit limit. If you own a credit card and your credit limit is $1,000, then your spending power is according to or determined by that limit. Once you reach your limit, you have no more spending power. Paul is stating that the credit limit on the power available to us is the amount of power released in the resurrection of Christ. How much power is that? Lawrence Richards said concerning this passage:

> "Paul piled up synonyms to emphasize the overwhelming nature of that divine power which had its fullest demonstration in the raising of Christ from the dead. The words Paul used include *dynamis* (intrinsic capability), *energeia* (effective power in action), *kratos* (power exerted to control and overcome resistance), and *ischys* (the vital power inherent in life)."[5]

Paul says it another way later in the same letter:

> Now to him who is able to do immeasurably more than all we ask or imagine, according to his power that is at work within us . . .
>
> EPHESIANS 3:20

Here again Paul piled on synonyms to express the immensity of this power that is available to us by faith. Paul started with the root word, *perissos*, which means "superabundant in quantity, excessive, and beyond measure." It is the same word Luke used to describe the twelve leftover baskets after Jesus multiplied the loaves and fishes. It is a word that means more than enough of whatever you need. For example, if you need-

---

[5] *Lawrence Richards, The Victor Bible Background Commentary.*

ed $20,000 to buy a car and you had $21,000, you would have *perissos*—more than enough.

Paul then added the prefix, *huper*, which means "over, beyond, and above." (We get our word "hyper" from this word.) When you add this prefix, the word now means "way beyond; superabundant in quantity." Continuing our example, you now have $100,000 to buy that $20,000 car.

But Paul is not finished. He tacked on the prefix, *ek*, which intensifies whatever word it goes with. Then, for good measure, he threw in an extra *huper* just in case we didn't get his meaning! Using our metaphor, we now have all the money in the world to buy our $20,000 car.

The exciting thing about this power is where it is located. It is within us. Colossians 1:29 says . . .

> To this end I strenuously contend with all the energy Christ so *powerfully works in me*. (NIV)

> For this purpose also I labor, striving according to His power, which *mightily works within me*. (NASB)

> That's why I work and struggle so hard, depending on *Christ's mighty power that works within me*. (NLT)

> . . . for which also I labour, striving according to *his working that is working in me* in power. (YLT)

> For this I toil, striving with all *the energy* which *He mightily inspires within me*. (RSV)

This is my work, and I can do it only because *Christ's mighty energy is at work within me.* (TLB)

To do this, I work and struggle, using *Christ's great strength that works so powerfully in me.* (NCV)

Smith Wigglesworth[6] used to say, "I am a thousand times bigger on the inside than I am on the outside." God's great power working in us by faith enables us to accomplish His work.

Conclusion

In this chapter, we have begun to examine why faith is so important. In the next chapter, we will continue to look at other reasons we need faith.

---

[6] *Smith Wigglesworth was an English preacher who was very influential in the early history of Pentecostalism. He is sometimes referred to as the "Apostle of Faith."*

APPLICATION

Discuss

1. Why should you understand the reasons you need faith? What practical difference will it make in your life?

_____

_____

_____

2. Give an example from a recent experience where you saw one of these three reasons you need faith working in your life. What did you learn through that experience?

_____

_____

_____

3. Which of the three reasons discussed in this chapter stood out to you as needing the most attention in your life? Why? What action step can you take to apply what you have understood?

_____

_____

_____

4. Do you have a spare tire mentality about faith? If so, why? What can you do to change your attitude and adopt the biblical attitude to live by faith?

_____

_____

_____

5. Have you ever been guilty of trying to do God's work in your own natural strength? Why was it difficult to have faith in God's power in that situation? What did you learn about yourself through that situation, and what can you do to make sure it doesn't happen again?

_____

_____

_____

Act

Read Paul's letter to the Galatians and look for every reference to the words *faith*, *believe*, or *believing*. (There are more than twenty.) Record the thoughts and insights God gives you.

Memorize

And without faith it is impossible to please God, because anyone who comes to him must believe that he exists and that he rewards those who earnestly seek him.

HEBREWS 11:6

CHAPTER 3

Why do We Need Faith?
Part 2

In the last chapter, we said that faith was important because we need it to please God, to live by, and to do God's work. In this chapter, we will conclude with five more reasons why we need faith.

We need faith to experience God's righteousness.

One of the most startling revelations of the New Testament is that God has made us righteous. This righteousness is found in Christ and is appropriated by faith.

> This righteousness is given through faith in Jesus Christ to all who believe. . . .
>
> ROMANS 3:22

Righteousness is the result of the judicial act of God, by which He pardons the sins of all those who believe in Christ, and accounts us as righteous in the eyes of the law. The law is not relaxed or set aside, but declared fulfilled in the strictest and most complete sense.[1] This is the act of a judge and not of a sovereign. A sovereign can set aside the law, but a judge cannot.

This is an important idea to understand. Righteousness is not God acting as a sovereign and setting aside the law to arbitrarily pardon guilty sinners. Righteousness is God acting like

---

[1] *Adapted from the* Illustrated Bible Dictionary, *M.G. Eaton, 401.*

a judge and declaring that in Christ we have perfectly fulfilled all the requirements of the divine law.

A ruler may sovereignly declare a guilty man innocent, but a judge cannot. For example, before leaving office, former American President Bill Clinton exercised the sovereign right of his office and granted a presidential pardon to Marc Rich, a billionaire commodities trader who had fled to Switzerland to avoid prosecution for income tax evasion and racketeering. The presidential pardon was not based on the merit or righteousness of Marc Rich. He was still guilty, but the law was set aside. This was the act of a sovereign, not a judge.

By contrast, the doctrine of righteousness declares that the law of God was fulfilled completely and totally in Christ. Therefore, the benefits God confers upon us are now based on our perfect obedience to the law—an obedience fulfilled in Christ and not in ourselves. God treats us as if we have perfectly obeyed every detail of His law—because we have—in Christ. Righteousness is not forgiveness. It is a declaration that we have perfectly satisfied the law forever.

This righteousness is the righteousness of Christ, and it is received by faith. This was the official doctrine of the Protestant Reformation. Martin Luther said:

"Jesus Christ died for our sins and was raised again for our justification. He alone is the Lamb of God who takes away the sins of the world. All have sinned and are justified freely, without their own works and merits, by His grace, through the redemption that is in Christ Jesus, in His blood. It is clear and certain that this faith alone justifies us."[2]

---

[2] *Martin Luther, The Smalcald Articles, Part Two, Article One.*

Not only was this the official doctrine of the Reformation, it has also been the informed view of the Church throughout history. Here are the words of some of the early Fathers of the Church:

Justin Martyr: "O unexpected benefit ... that the righteousness of One should justify many transgressors."[3]

John Chrysostom: "He made a righteous Person to be sin, in order that he might make sinners righteous ... it is the righteousness of God, when we are justified, not by works . . . but by grace, where all sin is made to vanish away."[4]

Augustine of Hippo: "We conclude that a man is not justified by the precepts of a holy life, but by faith in Jesus Christ."[5]

The person who is made righteous is entitled to all the advantages and rewards arising from perfect obedience to the law.

"I look to the Old Testament and I see certain blessings attached to the Covenant of Works and I say to myself by faith, 'Those blessings are mine, for I have kept the Covenant of Works in the Person of my Covenant Head and Surety. Every blessing which is promised to perfect obedience belongs to me, since I present to God a perfect obedience in the Person of my great Representative, the Lord Jesus Christ.'"[6]

---

[3] *Justin Martyr's* Letter to Diognetus *(circa second century).*

[4] Chrysostom Commentary on 2 Corinthians *(circa fourth century).*

[5] *Augustine,* On the Spirit and the Letter, *Chapter XXII (circa fifth century).*

[6] *Charles Spurgeon,* The Tenderness of Jesus, *Sermon #2148, June 8, 1890.*

The sole condition for this righteousness is faith. Faith is called a *condition* because it is the instrument by which the soul appropriates Christ and His righteousness. Therefore, faith does not earn righteousness, it receives it.[7]

Paul spent a good part of his ministry combating men who insisted that faith in Christ was insufficient and that adherence to the Mosaic Law was required for right standing with God. These men followed after Paul's ministry and tried to force his converts to receive circumcision. There was no other group that incited Paul to anger like these people. He warned the Galatians and the Philippians:

> But even if we or an angel from heaven should preach a gospel other than the one we preached to you, let them be under God's curse! As we have already said, so now I say again: If anybody is preaching to you a gospel other than what you accepted, let them be under God's curse![8]
>
> GALATIANS 1:8,9

> Watch out for those dogs, those evildoers, those mutilators of the flesh.
>
> PHILIPPIANS 3:2

Those people stirred righteous indignation so fervently in Paul because they vilified the work of Christ through their assertion that righteousness came through human effort. Paul knew that if anyone could qualify for righteousness based on

---

[7] *Adapted from the* Illustrated Bible Dictionary, *M.G. Easton, 401.*

[8] *"Paul knows that he has just made what some will consider an extreme statement [in verse 8]. But it is a deliberate one and not mere excitement. He will stand by it to the end. He calls down a curse on any one who proclaims a gospel to them contrary to that which they had received from him."* (Word Pictures in the New Testament)

works and not on faith, it was certainly himself. He had an impressive religious resumé.

> …though I myself have reasons for such confidence. If someone else thinks they have reasons to put confidence in the flesh, I have more: circumcised on the eighth day, of the people of Israel, of the tribe of Benjamin, a Hebrew of Hebrews; in regard to the law, a Pharisee; as for zeal, persecuting the church; as for righteousness based on the law, faultless.
>
> PHILIPPIANS 3:4-6

Paul makes an astonishing statement when he says he was faultless by the standards of legalistic righteousness. Who else could make such a claim? But was Paul's righteousness enough? Hardly.

> What is more, I consider everything a loss because of the surpassing worth of knowing Christ Jesus my Lord, for whose sake I have lost all things. I consider them garbage, that I may gain Christ and be found in him, not having a righteousness of my own that comes from the law, but that which is through faith in Christ—the righteousness that comes from God on the basis of faith.
>
> PHILIPPIANS 3:8,9

Paul uses an interesting Greek word in this passage, one that is sanitized considerably by most English translators: *skubalon*. The NIV translates it as "garbage," but the literal translation should be "the excrement of dogs." This is a fitting description of all our attempts to achieve the righteousness of God through our own efforts!

This same spiritual force that energized Paul's enemies to seek righteousness through human effort is still with us today. It effectively seduced many of the Galatians. Paul wrote:

> You unthinking and foolish Galatians! Who has put the evil eye on you? Have you taken leave of your senses? For it's obvious that you no longer have the crucified Jesus in clear focus. His sacrifice on the cross was certainly set before you clearly enough. Let me ask you this one question: How did your new life begin? Was it by working your heads off to please God? Or was it by hearing and believing God's Message? Are you going to continue this insanity? For only crazy people would think they could complete by their own efforts what was begun by God. If you weren't smart enough or strong enough or good enough to start it, how do you suppose you could finish it?
>
> GALATIANS 3:1-3[9]

It has also seduced many throughout the history of the Church. Why is this tendency to establish our own righteousness so strong within us? Because it feeds our ego. If righteousness is a free gift and there's nothing we can do to earn it, then we are more flawed than we would like to believe. And as long as we still have a human ego, we will have to fight this force.

The following example may help illustrate my point. Imagine these two different scenarios:

---

[9] *This passage is a conflation of several versions.*

John Q. Christian's alarm clock goes off at 4:30 on a Saturday morning, and he immediately rises to start his devotions. After two hours of prayer and two more hours of Bible reading, he rushes off to the local shopping mall for a day of witnessing. By 10:30 that evening, he has led three people to Christ. He finally arrives home about midnight and falls immediately into bed.

Jim Q. Christian's alarm clock goes off at around noon on the same Saturday morning. Instead of rousing from his slumber, he hits the snooze button seventeen consecutives times—aiming for a world record! He finally forces himself from the bed to his couch, snagging the television remote in the process. He spends the rest of the day in mindless channel surfing, interspersed with large quantities of pizza, ice cream, and soda. About midnight, as his friend John is returning from his labors at the mall, Jim crawls back to his room and falls immediately to sleep.

Which one of these scenarios reflects a biblical righteousness?

The answer is, of course, we do not know. Righteousness is not based on works, it is based on faith, and we do not know which of these men was exercising faith. It is possible to do all the things John did for the express purpose of gaining God's favor. It is also possible to do all the things Jim did by faith. This usually comes as a great shock to the average Christian, but it is true.

Certainly God wants us to live right and walk in holiness—but holiness should be the fruit of a life of faith and not the motivation for God's favor. This is often difficult to grasp because so much of our lives are oriented around performance. Do well at work and you receive a performance bonus. Do well in school and you get high grades. Do well on the team and you get the trophies. This seems normal, reasonable, and fair. But it is not the way of the kingdom of God.

However, God does not want sloppiness or our second best. He is a God of excellence. Everything He does is always first-class, and we should reflect that in every area of our lives. But it should come out of a heart of gratitude and faith and a desire to honor God—not because we feel we can gain His approval if we do.

We need faith to give glory to God.

> Yet he did not waver through unbelief regarding the promise of God, but was strengthened in his faith and *gave glory to God*, being fully persuaded that God had power to do what he had promised.
>
> ROMANS 4:20,21

Abraham's strong faith gave glory to God. John Piper, describing this passage, said:

> "Giving glory to God does not mean adding to God's glory. It does not mean improving upon God's gloriousness. It does mean calling attention to God's glory, showing it to be what it really is. Giving glory to God is making Him look real good."[10]

I remember being at the public swimming pool as a small boy many years ago in my hometown of Collinsville, Illinois. My family and friends were there and everyone seemed to be

---

[10] *John Piper,* In Hope Against Hope for the Glory of God, *sermon given on September 26, 1999.*

having a great time. But I was hesitant to enter the water, since it looked so cold, scary, and a little too deep. My father, standing in water barely up to his waist, beckoned me to jump. He stood a little back from the edge and promised to catch me.

At that moment, I had the opportunity to make my dad look really good. If I immediately and unhesitantly jumped in, all those around us would see that he was a trustworthy father. My faith in him would make him look good. It would, in a very small way, give glory to him. But if I hesitated, balked, or demonstrated excessive reluctance, it might have the opposite effect. It might make him look bad. My unwillingness to believe him would reflect one of three possible reasons:[11]

- Possibility #1: I thought he was unable to catch me; he wasn't strong enough.
- Possibility #2: I thought he was untrustworthy and wouldn't catch me; he didn't love me enough.
- Possibility #3: I thought he had a bad plan that wouldn't work; he wasn't smart enough.

When we demonstrate strong faith in God, we make Him look powerful. We declare to the world that He is strong enough to do what He said He would do. When we demonstrate strong faith in God, we make Him look loving. We declare to the world that He cares enough to meet our every need. When we demonstrate strong faith in God, we make Him look wise. We declare to the world that His plans are always the best plans.

The more impossible the promise of God looks, the better He looks when it finally comes to pass. When Abraham chose to

---

[11] *This story really happened to me, but the application of it was inspired by John Piper's sermon. For those who care, I did eventually jump.*

believe God in the midst of impossible circumstances, he made God look very good. That is what it means to give glory to God.

We need faith for answered prayers.

Jesus has given us some magnificent and astonishing promises concerning prayer. All effective prayer is based on a strong confidence in these promises.

> "If you believe, you will receive *whatever* you ask for in prayer."
>
> MATTHEW 21:22

> "And I will do *whatever* you ask in my name, so that the Father may be glorified in the Son. You may ask me for *anything* in my name, and I will do it."
>
> JOHN 14:13,14

> ". . . my Father will give you *whatever* you ask in my name. . . . Ask and *you will receive*, and your joy will be complete."
>
> JOHN 16:23,24

> This is the confidence we have in approaching God: that if we ask *anything* according to his will, he hears us. And if we know that he hears us—*whatever* we ask—we know that we have what we asked of him.
>
> 1 JOHN 5:14,15[12]

---

[12] *Sometimes people get hung up over this question, "But how do we know His will?" The answer is simple: Whatever is recorded in Scripture is His will. "For no matter how many promises God has made, they are 'Yes' in Christ" (2 Corinthians 1:20). To have the confidence John is referring to, find Bible verses that address the thing that you want. Meditate on them until you are convinced that they are for you.*

". . . all things for which you pray and ask, believe that you have received them, and they shall be granted you."

Mark 11:24 (NASB)[13]

These verses make it plain that faith is an essential prerequisite for answered prayer.

George Muller[14] recounted an incident he experienced while crossing the Atlantic on an ocean liner to an engagement in Quebec, Canada. During the voyage, the ship encountered a severe fog that threatened to delay its arrival. Muller found the Captain and said, "I must be in Quebec on Saturday."

When the Captain told him his request was impossible, Muller responded, "I have never missed an engagement in fifty-seven years; let us go to the chart room and pray."

Once in the chart room, the incredulous Captain said, "Mr. Muller, do you know how dense the fog is?"

"No," Muller said, "my eye is not on the fog, but on God who controls every circumstance of my life." He then knelt and said a simple, faith-filled prayer.

When he finished, the Captain knelt and began to pray also. Muller stopped him, saying, "As you do not believe, there is no need for you to pray. Get up, Captain, open the door and you will find the fog has lifted."

The Captain did as he was instructed only to see that the fog had lifted. George Muller made his engagement in Quebec on time.

---

[13] The New Commentary on the Whole Bible *says about this verse, "The verb for* receive *in the Greek is an aorist tense, which is always used to describe an accomplished past action. The Christian whose faith is of that quality that he believes he has "already received it" when he asks, will discover that he actually has it. This verse sets out how far a person's faith can reach."*

[14] *George Muller (1805-1898) was a minister who cared for orphans in Bristol, England. He never made requests for financial support and never went into debt, but he cared for over 10,000 orphans during his lifetime.*

Another example from George Muller's diary shows the importance of persistent faith in prayer:

> "In November 1844, I began to pray for the conversion of five individuals. I prayed every day without a single intermission, whether sick or in health, on the land, on the sea, and whatever the pressure of my engagements might be. Eighteen months elapsed before the first of the five was converted. I thanked God and prayed on for the others. Five years elapsed, and then the second was converted. I thanked God for the second, and prayed on for the other three. Day by day, I continued to pray for them, and six years passed before the third was converted. I thanked God for the three, and went on praying for the other two."

These two remained unconverted. Thirty-six years later, he wrote that although the other two were still not converted, "But I hope in God, I pray on, and look for the answer. They are not converted yet, but they will be." In 1897, fifty-two years after he began to pray, these two men were finally converted—after Muller died.[15]

We need faith to receive the promises of God.

God's Word is filled with promises, but they generally will not come to us unless we actively believe. The writer of Hebrews confirmed this when he wrote:

> We do not want you to become lazy, but to imitate those who through faith and patience inherit what has been promised.

> HEBREWS 6:12

---

[15] *Ben Patterson,* Deepening Your Conversation with God, *105,106.*

Notice that we do not inherit the promises just because they are ours. We have to supply faith and patience in order to inherit them. Paul wrote to Timothy:

> . . . Take hold of the eternal life to which you were called . . .
>
> 1 TIMOTHY 6:12

Our English phrase "take hold" is translated from the Greek word *epilambanomai*, which means "to seize, lay hold of, or take possession of." It comes from a metaphor drawn from the act of seizing someone with both hands to rescue him from peril.[16] It is a very active and aggressive word, and it clearly implies that if we want to experience God's promises, we must take hold of them with a violent and aggressive faith.

On September 4, 1987, Henry Dempsey was flying a commuter jet about 4,000 feet above the Atlantic Ocean from Maine to Boston. He heard a rattling sound toward the rear of the plane, and leaving the controls to his co-pilot, he went to investigate. As he approached the tail section, the plane hit turbulence and he was thrown forward against the rear door.

The door was hinged at the bottom but not latched properly. When Dempsey crashed against the door, it opened and sucked him out of the plane. The co-pilot saw the 'door ajar' indicator light flash on and immediately requested an emergency landing at the nearest airport. He radioed the Coast Guard and asked for a search and rescue operation for a pilot who had fallen out of the plane.

---

[16] *Thayer's Greek Lexicon.*

But the rescue was not needed. The moment Dempsey had tumbled out of the plane, he seized the outdoor ladder railings. He held on for ten minutes upside down with only his feet inside the plane. When they landed, his head was twelve inches from the ground.

When the rescue workers arrived, he could not let go of the rail. He had seized it so tightly that it took more than fifteen minutes for the workers to pry his hands free. Henry Dempsey's amazing rescue vividly portrays the essence of *epilambanomai*. He seized the ladder railings the way we must seize the promises of God.

We need faith to resist the devil.[17]

We have a real enemy, and he is playing for keeps.

> . . . Your enemy the devil prowls around like a roaring lion looking for someone to devour. Resist him, standing firm in the faith . . .
>
> 1 PETER 5:8,9

We will not be able to resist the devil apart from a strong, assertive faith.

Smith Wigglesworth was once at a bus stop with several others waiting for a bus. The door of a nearby house opened and out stepped a very proper elderly woman. As she approached the bus stop, she became aware that her little dog had left the house and was following her. She immediately implored her dog in the sweetest tones to return home. After much cajoling, the dog finally acquiesced. However, as soon as she turned toward the bus stop, the dog began following her again. The woman

---

[17] *We will examine this topic in great depth in the second book.*

entreated her puppy as sweetly as possible, and once again he consented. But as soon as she turned her back, the dog began following her again. Finally, after several more rounds with the dog, the woman stomped her foot with authority and shouted, "Scat!" The dog tucked his tail between his legs, scurried home, and was not seen again. Without a moment's hesitation, Wigglesworth bellowed, "That's how you have to talk to the devil!"

Martin Luther would talk to the devil just like that. He once said:

> "By faith in Christ a person may gain such sure and sound comfort, that he need not fear the devil, sin, death, or any evil. 'Sir Devil,' he may say, 'I am not afraid of you. I have a Friend whose name is Jesus Christ, in whom I believe. He has abolished the Law, condemned sin, vanquished death, and destroyed hell for me. He is bigger than you, Satan. He has licked you, and holds you down. You cannot hurt me.' This is the faith that overcomes the devil."[18]

Everything of value in God's kingdom comes at a great cost.[19] Part of that cost is the opposition from our spiritual enemy who will do everything possible to stop us from experiencing God's best. Faith is of great value. Therefore, we should expect that it will come at a great cost and that it will require a great fight. In order to remain in that fight and persevere in the quest for faith, we must be aware of the benefits and value

---

[18] *Martin Luther,* Commentary on Galatians.

[19] *Cost is measured by value. There is a great cost obtaining anything in God's Kingdom, but the value is so great, the cost seems small in comparison. "The kingdom of heaven is like a merchant looking for fine pearls. When he found one of great value, he went away and sold everything he had and bought it" (Matthew 13:45,46). The pearl was costly, but in comparison to its value, it was the deal of a lifetime.*

of faith. We need to know why we need faith if we are to pursue it diligently—and to hold on to it in the midst of opposition and pressure.

Conclusion

We have examined the eight reasons we need faith. In the next chapter, we will look at what faith is.

APPLICATION

Discuss

1. Is biblical righteousness the result of God acting as a sovereign or as a judge? Why does it matter? What difference will it make in your life?

_____

_____

_____

2. Many Christians find it difficult to experience God's righteousness. They know it is the truth and that it is an important doctrine of the Church, but it just doesn't seem real to them. Why do you think that is? Have you felt that way at times in your life? Why? What can you do about it?

_____

_____

_____

3. How strong is the faith component of your prayer life? Why? What can you do to make it stronger?

_____

_____

_____

4. Faith takes an aggressive attitude towards God's promises. How do you rank on the passive/aggressive scale? Are you as aggressive in laying hold of God's promises as you should be? Why? What can you do to increase your aggressiveness?

_____

_____

_____

Act

Read the account of Jesus' dealings with the devil in Matthew 4:1-11 and Luke 4:1-13. Record all the principles and insights concerning faith you can find in this event.

Memorize

Yet he did not waver through unbelief regarding the promise of God, but was strengthened in his faith and gave glory to God, being fully persuaded that God had power to do what he had promised.

ROMANS 4:20,21

CHAPTER 4

What is Faith?
Part 1

I n these next few chapters, we will try to understand what faith is. In order to help us comprehend the essence of faith, looking at what faith is not will be helpful. We will examine three common substitutes for faith: hope, knowledge, and presumption.

Hope

In order to understand what the Bible teaches about hope, we must first understand that we use the word differently. Sometimes we use it to refer to wishful thinking or strong desire. For example, someone might ask, "Are you going to get that raise?" You might respond, "I sure hope so." Your response is just another way of saying, "I am not confident it will happen, but I sure want it to."

While this is a valid use of the word, the Bible does not use it that way. In fact, that is the exact opposite of how the Bible uses it. Biblical hope is a firm assurance about things that are unseen and still in the future. It is the climate that faith works in. It is the dream, desire, or goal that we expect to receive. It is the confident expectation of good things to come. Hope starts the process of faith by painting a vivid image of what could be. Then faith goes to work. Hope is an important part of our life of faith, but it is not faith.

One of the most important distinctions between faith and hope is that hope always lives in the future tense.

> ... But hope that is seen is no hope at all. Who hopes for what they already have? But if we hope for what we do not yet have, we wait for it patiently.
>
> ROMANS 8:24,25

There are many benefits to a strong, Bible-based hope. Here are a few.

Hope activates our faith.

> Against all hope, Abraham in hope believed and so became the father of many nations ...
>
> ROMANS 4:18

The God's Word Bible translates this verse, *When there was nothing left to hope for, Abraham still hoped and believed* ... The Weymouth translation says, *Under utterly hopeless circumstances he hopefully believed* ... The New American Standard Bible says, *In hope against hope he believed* ...

Abraham kept a strong Bible-based hope long after all natural hope was gone. His confident expectation and firm assurance of God's promise stimulated and activated his faith. He saw the promise clearly, and would not waver when everything around him said there was no hope left.

Hope fuels our endurance.

> We remember before our God and Father . . . your
> endurance inspired by hope in our Lord Jesus Christ.
> 1 THESSALONIANS 1:3

In the early morning hours of July 4, 1952, Florence Chadwick dove into the Pacific Ocean off Catalina Island. She intended to swim the twenty-plus miles to the California coast. Chadwick was already an accomplished long-distance swimmer. Two years earlier, she had crossed the English Channel in both directions—the first woman to ever accomplish that feat.

But the conditions that day were not in her favor. The water was icy, the fog nearly impenetrable. She could barely see the boat she was supposed to follow. Several times, her team drove sharks away with rifle fire. After fifteen hours in the water, she gave out. Her trainer urged her on—they were so close. But all she could see was fog. She quit—one mile from her goal. She said later, "If I could have seen the land I might have made it."

Two months later in clear weather, Florence swam the channel successfully, setting a new speed record. There was no fog, and she could clearly see her goal. Because the land was in sight, she endured to the end.

That is what hope does for us.

The author of Hebrews reinforces this idea when he exhorts us to follow the example of Jesus, who endured the cross because of the joy that was set before Him. If we fix our eyes on Him, the author says, we will not grow weary and lose heart. This is a clear reference to the athletic competitions of Greece. The races were laid out on a straight track with the spectators on either side. The judge sat at the finish line holding the laurel wreath for the winner. From the start of the race to the finish, the competitors could see the prize. If they kept their eyes focused on it, they could find the strength to endure.

A clear and detailed hope enables us to endure obstacles and press on to the finish line.

Hope anchors our soul.

> We have this hope as an anchor for the soul, firm and secure. . . .
>
> HEBREWS 6:19

Albert Barnes, commenting on this verse in his *Notes on the New Testament*, said:

> "Hope accomplishes for the soul the same thing an anchor does for a ship. It makes it secure. An anchor preserves a ship when the waves beat and the wind blows, and as long as the anchor holds, so long the ship is safe. So with the soul of the Christian. In the tempests and trials of life, his mind is calm as long as his hope is firm."

There are many more advantages that hope brings into our lives. But as valuable as it is, hope is not faith. We should not get these two confused, or we may substitute hope for faith.

Knowledge

Knowledge is another important part of our faith life, but knowledge is not faith. Faith begins with knowledge—you have to know God's Word before you can believe it—but it does not end there. Knowledge is believing with the intellect; faith is believing with the heart. Knowledge that enters your mind must drop the all-important eighteen inches from your head to your heart.

> For it is with your heart that you believe . . .
>
> ROMANS 10:10

Knowledge is mentally agreeing with the truth of the Bible without personally appropriating it by faith. John Wesley once said, "The devil has given the Church a counterfeit to faith—mental assent." Mental assent is head knowledge. It is agreeing with the Word of God in the mind without believing it in the heart. Knowledge is the starting point of faith, but if knowledge is not appropriated, it remains mental assent. Mark 4 gives us a good picture of mental assent.

> That day when evening came, he said to his disciples, "Let us go over to the other side."
>
> MARK 4:35

The Gospel writers do not always give us chronological information in their accounts, but when they do, we should take note because the information is important—a clue to understanding what is happening in the scene. When Mark tells us that the event he is about to describe took place on "that day," he wants us to know that the prior events of that day have special significance concerning what is about to happen. We must then ask, "What was so special about that day?"

Jesus had spent that day teaching about the Word of God and the power it has in the life of a person who receives it by faith. The disciples had listened to Jesus speak the Word the entire day. They were saturated with the Word, and they were more than ready for the faith challenge that was yet to come that night. Jesus knew it was coming and so He prepared His disciples in advance. He had taught them that day that the devil comes immediately to steal the Word, and He knew that the storm they were about to experience was demonically inspired to steal the Word of God out of their hearts. He wanted them to be ready.

> Leaving the crowd behind, they took him along, just as he was, in the boat. There were also other boats with him. A furious squall came up, and the waves broke over the boat, so that it was nearly swamped.
>
> MARK 4:36,37

All the disciples but one were from Galilee, and they knew about storms on that sea. The particular location of the Sea of Galilee makes it susceptible to sudden and fierce storms. The surface of the water is almost 700 feet below sea level and the sea is surrounded on several sides by high hills. Cool air from these highlands rushes down the gorges and ravines and strikes the water with intense violence. Because the disciples had lived near its shores, it is very possible that they each knew someone who had drowned in a storm just like the one they were experiencing. Their terror was understandable.

> Jesus was in the stern, sleeping on a cushion. The disciples woke him and said to him, "Teacher, don't you care if we drown?" He got up, rebuked the wind and said to the waves, "Quiet! Be still!" Then the wind

William Ewing, writing in the International Standard Bible Encyclopedia, *tells this story about his experience with the Sea of Galilee. "Twice in over five years the present writer witnessed such a hurricane. Once it burst from the South. In a few moments the air was thick with mist, through which one could hear the roar of the tortured waters. In about ten minutes the wind fell as suddenly as it had risen. The air cleared, and the wide welter of foam-crested waves attested the fury of the blast. On the second occasion the wind blew from the East, and the phenomena described above were practically repeated."*

died down and it was completely calm. He said to his disciples, "Why are you so afraid? Do you still have no faith?"

MARK 4:38-40

Faith can sleep in a storm, but unbelief is always troubled.

We see this truth illustrated in an incident that happened to John Wesley during a sea voyage to America. A huge storm buffeted the ship, and a wave broke over the deck and split the main sail in pieces. Wesley recorded in his diary, "A terrible screaming began among the English, but the German Moravians calmly sang on." Wesley was deeply impressed that even the women and children manifested no fear but were perfectly calm. He concluded about himself, "I have a fair summer religion; I can talk well . . . and believe while no danger is near. But let death stare me in the face and my spirit is troubled."

The disciples were like John Wesley that day, they forgot everything Jesus had preached and immediately reverted to fear and worry. They even challenged the character of God by accusing Jesus of not caring.

If faith comes by hearing, you would expect that a full day of hearing Jesus preach the Word would produce a certain level of faith. That is why Jesus said to His disciples after He rebuked the storm, "Do you still have no faith?" How could the people who heard the Word all day end up with no faith? Martin Luther once said in his *Commentary on Paul's Epistle to the Galatians*:

> "If it were not for the example of the Galatian churches, I would never have thought it possible that anybody who had received the Word of God with such eagerness as they had could so quickly let go of it."

The disciples certainly did. Jesus said they had no faith. There are a few adjectives Jesus used to describe the faith of people He encountered during His ministry. On two occasions, He used the adjective "great."

> Then Jesus answered, "Woman, you have *great* faith! Your request is granted." And her daughter was healed at that moment.
>
> MATTHEW 15:28

> When Jesus heard this, he was amazed at him [the Centurion], and turning to the crowd following him, he said, "I tell you, I have not found such *great* faith even in Israel."
>
> LUKE 7:9

Matthew used the Greek word *megas* to describe the Syrophoenician woman's faith. The word means "of considerable size, number, quantity, magnitude, or extent." Luke used the Greek word *tosoutos* to describe the Centurion's faith. The word means "vast in quantity and amount; large; notably above the average in size or magnitude." If Jesus ever describes your faith, you want Him to use one of these words!

But there were several times when Jesus could not describe His disciples' faith with those words. In those cases, He used the adjective "little."

> Immediately Jesus reached out his hand and caught him. "You of *little* faith," he said, "why did you doubt?"
> MATTHEW 14:31

> "If that is how God clothes the grass of the field, which is here today, and tomorrow is thrown into the fire, how much more will he clothe you—you of *little* faith!"
> LUKE 12:28

Both Matthew and Luke used the Greek word *oligos*. The word means "puny in extent or degree; of inferior size, strength, or significance." It is definitely not as good as *great faith*—but at least it is some faith. That is much better than how Jesus described the disciples' faith on the day we are discussing: *no faith*. None. Nada. Zip. Nil. The disciples had listened to the Word all day and had received no faith. It was all head knowledge. It was all mental assent.

Mental assent is passive and superficial, and it produces no lasting change in us. It only fools us into thinking that we have real faith. But difficult times and challenging circumstances always reveal what we actually believe. And Jesus has a way of arranging difficulties and challenges to help us see what is really in our hearts. He does not do this to shame us, but to give us a chance to replace the mental assent with true Bible faith. The following is a good example of the difference between mental assent and real Bible faith.

Charles Blondin (1824-1897) was one of the greatest acrobats of all time. Raised in a circus family, he began his training at five years of age. Within six months, he was astonishing crowds as "the Little Wonder." Blondin performed many dangerous feats during his career, but the most outstanding were his exhibitions on an 1100-foot-long tightrope stretched 160 feet above Niagara Falls. He crossed the Falls several times, always with different theatrical variations: blindfolded, on stilts, pushing a wheelbarrow. Once, he even sat on the tightrope and cooked an omelet!

But his first crossing stands out above all the others. After successfully crossing Niagara, Blondin asked the gathered crowd, "Who believes I can cross back over the Falls?"

The crowd roared together, "We believe!"

"Then who," Blondin said, "is willing to get on my back while I cross?"

The crowd was silent. Finally, one brave man stepped out of the crowd and said, "I will."

He climbed on Blondin's shoulders, and they both walked successfully over Niagara Falls.

The crowd at Niagara Falls mentally assented to Blondin's ability to cross, but the brave man who climbed on his shoulders believed from his heart.

Presumption

Presumption is also not faith. But presumption is different from knowledge and hope because both knowledge and hope have a valid role in the life of faith, and presumption never does. Presumption is arrogant overconfidence. It is taking something for granted and supposing it is true without examination or proof. It is acting as if you know God's will when you have no scriptural evidence to support your supposition. The seven sons of Sceva provide us with a good example of presumption.

Extraordinary miracles were taking place in Ephesus. Many were being healed. Demons were coming out of people. Handkerchiefs that Paul had prayed over were even being placed on demonized people and the evil spirits were leaving. Sceva's boys presumed they could get in on the action.

> Some Jews who went around driving out evil spirits tried to invoke the name of the Lord Jesus over those who were demon-possessed. They would say, "In the name of the Jesus whom Paul preaches, I command you to come out." Seven sons of Sceva, a Jewish chief priest, were doing this. One day the evil spirit answered them, "Jesus I know, and Paul I know about, but who are you?" Then the man who had the evil spirit jumped on them and overpowered them all. He gave them such a beating that they ran out of the house naked and bleeding.
>
> Acts 19:13-16

Presumption can leave you naked and bleeding.

The Israelites also acted presumptuously when they were in the wilderness. In Numbers 14, the people believed the bad report the ten spies gave them about the Promised Land and threatened to stone Joshua and Caleb. They wanted to elect a new leader to take them back to Egypt. But God intervened and said to Moses:

> "How long will these people treat me with contempt? How long will they refuse to believe in me, in spite of all the miraculous signs I have performed among them?"
>
> NUMBERS 14:11

God relented from judging them because of Moses' intercession but declared that because of their unbelief and disobedience . . .

> ". . . not one of those who saw my glory and the signs I performed in Egypt and in the wilderness but who disobeyed me and tested me ten times—not one of them will ever see the land I promised on oath to their ancestors. No one who has treated me with contempt will ever see it."
>
> NUMBERS 14:22,23

The next day the people had a change of heart. Now they were ready to go. Now they were ready to obey. Now they were ready to believe. But what they thought was faith was really presumption. They were acting as if going to the Promised Land was God's will when they had no scriptural evidence to support their assumption. Actually, just the opposite was true, as they would soon discover.

Early the next morning they set out for the highest point in the hill country, saying, "Now we are ready to go up to the land the LORD promised. Surely we have sinned!" But Moses said, "Why are you disobeying the LORD's command? This will not succeed! Do not go up, because the LORD is not with you. You will be defeated by your enemies, for the Amalekites and the Canaanites will face you there. Because you have turned away from the LORD, he will not be with you and you will fall by the sword."

NUMBERS 14:40-43

But the people did go in spite of Moses' word to them. The results were predictable.

Nevertheless, in their *presumption* they went up toward the highest point in the hill country, though neither Moses nor the ark of the LORD's covenant moved from the camp. Then the Amalekites and the Canaanites who lived in that hill country came down and attacked them and beat them down all the way to Hormah.

NUMBERS 14:44,45

Presumption never ends well.

In the New Testament, James also warned us about acting presumptuously.

Now listen, you who say, "Today or tomorrow we will go to this or that city, spend a year there, carry on business and make money." Why, you do not even

> know what will happen tomorrow. What is your life? You are a mist that appears for a little while and then vanishes. Instead, you ought to say, "If it is the Lord's will, we will live and do this or that."
>
> JAMES 4:13-15

Why is this presumption? Because the person who is making these assertions about what he will do has no scriptural evidence to support them. He has no promise from God about what will happen tomorrow. He thinks he has faith, but he is instead arrogant and overconfident. Faith begins when the will of God is known, and if we do not know His will, all our boasting is just presumption.

I knew a young man who had recently come to faith in Christ. After listening to a stirring message on faith, he determined he would receive healing for his eyes. He prayed what he thought was a mighty faith prayer, took off his glasses, and threw them in a nearby dumpster. He was healed, he declared, and he had the corresponding action to prove it. Three days later, this young man, myself, and several friends spent a fruitless hour rummaging in that trash bin searching for his discarded glasses. We never found them, and he had to purchase new ones. He made the mistake of confusing activity with faith. He assumed that all he had to do was show God he believed by tossing his glasses away and then God would be obligated to heal his eyes. He confused presumption for faith.

Conclusion

If faith is not hope, mental assent, or presumption, then what is it? In the next two chapters, we will try to answer that question.

APPLICATION

Discuss

1. Hope is a clear picture of what you want God to do in and through your life. The clearer the picture, the stronger your hope. How clear is your picture and how strong is your hope? What can you do to strengthen it?

_____

_____

_____

2. God uses situations to reveal to us that what we thought was faith was only mental assent. What situations have you been in the last year that showed you how much mental assent you had? What did God teach you through those situations? How can you ensure that if a similar situation occurs, you will respond in true Bible faith and not with mere mental assent?

_____

_____

_____

3. Presumption is acting as if you know God's will when you have no scriptural evidence to support your supposition. Give a recent example of presumption in your life. What did God teach you through that event?

_____

_____

_____

Act

Using a concordance, Bible software, or online resource, look up ten verses from the New Testament concerning hope. Record your thoughts about each verse.

Memorize

We have this hope as an anchor for the soul, firm and secure. . . .

HEBREWS 6:19

CHAPTER 5

What is Faith?
Part 2

In the last chapter, we saw that faith is not hope, knowledge, or presumption. In this chapter and the next, we will examine what faith is.

Faith is a relationship with God.

First and foremost, faith is a relationship with God.

"Because of centuries of church tradition, we tend to think of faith in a creed, in a doctrine, in a form of theology, but it isn't; it is a relationship with God."[1]

Faith is not a formula, set of rules, or prescription. Faith is how we interact with God. Paul wrote to the Ephesians:

Because of Christ and our faith in him, we can now come boldly and confidently into God's presence.

EPHESIANS 3:12 (NLT)

Through faith, we may approach God with confidence and with full assurance. The writer of Hebrews urges us to approach God confidently through faith in what Jesus has accomplished for us. He said:

---

[1] *Derek Prince,* Faith Relates us to the Invisible, *Derek Prince Legacy Radio, November 17, 2008.*

> Therefore, brothers and sisters, since we have *confidence* to enter the Most Holy Place by the blood of Jesus, by a new and living way opened for us through the curtain, that is, his body, and since we have a great priest over the house of God, let us draw near to God with a sincere heart and with the full assurance that faith brings, having our hearts sprinkled to cleanse us from a guilty conscience and having our bodies washed with pure water.
>
> HEBREWS 10:19-22

> Let us then approach God's throne of grace with *confidence*, so that we may receive mercy and find grace to help us in our time of need.
>
> HEBREWS 4:16

Our English word "confidence" is derived from the Latin word *fides*, which means "faith," and the prefix *con* which means "with." Someone who is confident is someone *with faith*. The fact that the word is used in both of these passages concerning our relationship with God underscores how important faith is in that relationship.

It is significant that the writer refers to it as the throne of grace and not of judgment (although *God will judge the living and the dead*). He also did not call it the throne of truth (although God is true though *every human being a liar*), or the throne of righteousness (although *God is a righteous judge, a God who displays his wrath every day*). But he did call it the throne of grace, a throne where we draw near to *receive mercy and find grace to help us in our time of need*—which is every moment of every day. And this throne of grace is accessed by faith.

We also need to understand that faith is not a mere ticket to get us the things we want. Faith should not be seen as a ticket to get something, but more as a treasure of value. A ticket only has value for what it represents. Once we exchange it for the thing we really want, we simply discard it. A treasure, however, has intrinsic and lasting value.

For example, in 2009, a friend of mind gave me four tickets to watch the St. Louis Cardinals play the Chicago Cubs at Busch Stadium over the fourth of July weekend. To a lifetime Cardinal fan, things don't get much better than that, and I had great expectations about the game. First, because any chance to see my team play is always a treat. Second, because there has been a long-standing rivalry between the two teams (it is a requirement for all Cardinal fans to root against the Cubs). Third, because it was a holiday weekend, and the two clubs were locked in a feverish pennant race.

So these tickets were precious to me—but only for what they represented. Once they got me into the game (along with my dad and two sons), I discarded them. They no longer had any value.

But faith is not a ticket—an item to be discarded once you receive what you want. Faith is a relationship with God. And that is our treasure. As John Piper said:

> "To put it positively, 'belief' in Jesus is coming to Him to feed on Him; that is to get my satisfaction, to have my soul-thirst satisfied from Him."[2]

---

[2] Battling Unbelief Series, *faithbyhearing.wordpress.com.*

Faith is total trust in God's character.

The foundation of faith is the character of God. Because God is trustworthy, we can trust Him and have faith in Him.

> . . . if we are faithless, he remains faithful, for he cannot disown himself.
>
> 2 TIMOTHY 2:13

John Calvin declared that a right definition of faith must include the idea that it is a firm and certain knowledge of God's benevolence toward us. This certain knowledge of God's loving character is founded upon the truth of the freely given promise in Christ, both revealed to our minds and sealed upon our hearts through the Holy Spirit." The author of Hebrews tells us that:

> By faith even Sarah herself received ability to conceive, even beyond the proper time of life, since she considered Him faithful who had promised.
>
> HEBREWS 11:11 (NASB)

The word translated "considered" could be defined this way—"to think about carefully and thoroughly so as to form a proper judgment." Sarah carefully and thoroughly thought about the faithfulness of God, and the result was faith—total confidence in God's character.

A television program preceding the 1988 Winter Olympics featured blind skiers being trained for slalom skiing. Paired with sighted skiers, the blind skiers were taught on the flats how to make right and left turns. When that was mastered, they were taken to the slalom slope, where their sighted partners skied beside them shouting, "Left!" and "Right!" at the appropriate times. As they trusted and obeyed the sighted skiers, they were able to navigate the course and cross the finish line. They depended solely on the sighted skiers' word. It was either complete trust or catastrophe.

We are the blind skiers attempting to navigate the slippery slopes of life. But fortunately, we have a trustworthy guide whispering directions in our ears. If we trust Him, we will finish the course. And we can trust Him because He is perfect in integrity and worthy of our trust. Integrity is a rigid, unyielding, and steadfast adherence to the truth. Faith is impossible without it. Because God is perfect in integrity, we have a strong foundation for our confidence in God.

> "He who is the Glory of Israel does not lie or change his mind; for he is not a human being, that he should change his mind."
>
> 1 SAMUEL 15:29

> Let God be true, and every human being a liar. . . .
>
> ROMANS 3:4

> . . . it is impossible for God to lie . . .
>
> HEBREWS 6:18

John Paton (1824-1907) spent over forty-five years as a missionary to the New Hebrides in the South Pacific. When he was translating the New Testament into their native tongue, he struggled to find a comparable word in their language he could use for faith. The natives were cannibals that ate the flesh of their defeated foes. They practiced infanticide and widow sacrifice, killing the widows of deceased men so that they could serve their husbands in the next world. Their whole worship was one of slavish fear, and they had no idea of a God of mercy or grace.

One day a native ran up the stairs into Paton's house, rushed into his study, and flung himself on a chair. He said to the missionary, "It is good to rest my whole weight in this chair." Paton had found the word he would use for faith. Faith is resting your whole weight on God. Paton finished his translation shortly afterwards, and before he died testified that the entire island had been won to faith in Christ.

Because of God's absolute integrity, we can rest in total dependence upon what He has said He will do. When George Muller was asked what faith was, he replied:

> "What is faith? In the simplest manner in which I am able to express it, I answer: Faith is the assurance that the thing which God has said in His Word is true, and that God will act according to what He has said in His Word."[3]

God's Word is surer than that of a trusted friend. Martin Luther said:

> "Faith honors him whom it trusts with the most reverent and highest regard since it considers him truthful and trustworthy. There is no other honor equal to the estimate of truthfulness and righteousness with which we honor him whom we trust. . . . On the other hand, there is no way in which we can

---

[3] *Excerpt from a sermon by Muller entitled* Real Faith.

show greater contempt for a man than to regard him
as false and wicked and to be suspicious of him, as
we do when we do not trust him."[4]

That is why unbelief is a sin. It questions the character of
God and challenges His integrity. It impugns His character
and suggests that He is not dependable, and therefore, we cannot depend upon Him. But real faith rests confidently in God,
knowing that He is trustworthy and that He will perform what
He has spoken.

"Faith is the primary covenant requirement of God,
precisely because it humbles us and amplifies the
trustworthiness and all-sufficiency of God."[5]

Faith is complete confidence in God's written Word.

The author of Hebrews provides us with a succinct definition of what faith is:

Now faith is the assurance of things hoped for, the
conviction of things not seen.

HEBREWS 11:1 (NASB)

The word "assurance" derives from the Greek word *hupos-
tasis*, which means "that which stands under anything." It originally referred to the sediment or foundation under a building.
Faith is the foundation, the root, the underlying substance of
hope. In the first century, it was used as a legal term referring
to the transfer of property, and was commonly used in busi-

---

[4] Luther's Works, *Volume 31, 350.*
[5] *John Piper,* Preaching as Worship, *Trinity Journal, Spring 1995.*

ness documents as the basis or guarantee of transactions. It was essentially a title deed. So, Hebrews 11:1 could be reworded this way:

Faith is the 'title deed' of all the things we hope for.

A few illustrations from contemporary society may help clarify this concept.

If you make an offer on a piece of property and the owner accepts the offer, then you must wait while the proper legal documents are processed and the deal is closed before you can take possession of the property. While you are waiting for this process to conclude, someone might ask you, "Is that property yours?" You would have to say, "I hope so." You have a confident expectation that it will be yours soon, but it is not yours yet. But the day the paperwork is completed and your name is recorded on the title deed, then you can boldly say, "The property is mine." When you have the title deed, you have the property. The title deed is the assurance of the thing you had hoped for.

If you are about to graduate from college and your father calls to say he has bought you a new car, you would enthusiastically tell your friends. But some might be doubtful. They might say, "I don't see any car," or, "How do you know he really bought you a car?" However, the next day a special delivery package arrives with the title deed to a brand new car—and it has your name on it. As you wave the title deed in front of your skeptical friends, they now have to agree that you certainly have the car. They still can't see it, but they know you have it. It may still take a while for the actual car to arrive, since it has to be shipped from another state. But that is just logistics. You have the title deed, and it is just a matter of time before you will have the actual car.

Faith is the title deed, the assurance that what God has promised is yours—even if you cannot see it yet!

I received a bad report a number of years ago from a friend who had just come from the doctor's office. The physician had discovered a malignant tumor, and he was very concerned she would not live. I did not have sufficient time to prepare myself in prayer to respond to her situation, so I cast my care upon the Lord and planned a time when I could respond properly and in faith. The next day I set aside the necessary time for prayer. I began by building my faith through declaring every scriptural promise I knew that covered this case. I was determined not to pray for her until I had the title deed, the full assurance of what I was hoping for. I did not know how long it would take, but I knew that until I had the assurance, praying was pointless.

After an hour and a half of bold declaration and meditation, the assurance came. Describing this experience is difficult, but when the assurance comes, you know that you know you have it. I like to picture the doorbell ringing and the FedEx man delivering a package. Inside is the title deed, and the thing for which I have hoped is at last mine.

After you have assurance, prayer is easy. I prayed a simple thirty-second prayer, and waited for the good report that I knew would come. Within days, my friend called and said that the situation had resolved itself. (She was not a believer and did not understand what had really happened.)

Hebrews 11:1 also tells us that faith is the conviction of things not seen. The word "conviction" derives from the Greek word *elengchos*, a forensic term referring to a lawyer's presentation of irrefutable evidence in the courtroom. It was a word used in the criminal courts to describe the process by which a prosecutor would present evidence to prove to the jury that the criminal was guilty. The prosecutor would present the evidence so cogently and clearly that the jury would feel they had actually seen the crime, even though, of course, they had not.

Elengchos is a word that means someone is so convinced about something, he acts as though he has seen it with his own eyes, when in fact he has not. It is evidential proof that produces an unshakeable confidence. As Charles Spurgeon said:

> "If God has spoken to us in the Scriptures and revealed a truth that has no analogy in nature, that is not supported by the judgment of learned men, and to which our own experience seems to be in contradiction, still God must be believed. The fact that God has said it should weigh the scales of our understanding. Surely you are not going to set the evidence of your eyes against the declaration of God who cannot lie. I am determined that if my senses contradict God, I would rather deny every one of them than believe that God could lie."[6]

Faith is obedience to God.

The Bible makes a direct connection between obedience and faith. Paul said that God had given him grace and apostleship to call people from among *all the Gentiles to the obedience that comes from faith* (Romans 1:5). In the same letter he first told the Romans that their faith was *being reported all over the*

---

[6] *Robert Hall, ed. The Triumph of Faith in a Believer's Life, 80.*

world (Romans 1:8). Then he told them that *everyone has heard about your obedience* (Romans 16:19). Obviously faith and obedience were synonymous to Paul.

The writer to the Hebrews also made the same connection between faith and obedience when he described what happened to the Israelites who followed Moses out of Egypt. He first states that the Israelites could not enter the Promised Land because of their disobedience.

> And to whom did God swear that they would never enter his rest if not to those who disobeyed?
>
> HEBREWS 3:18

Then, in the next verse, he states that they could not enter the Promised Land because of unbelief.

> So we see that they were not able to enter, because of their unbelief.
>
> HEBREWS 3:19

Apparently, the author saw unbelief and disobedience as synonymous concepts.

We see examples of this all through Scripture. When God told Samuel to go to Jesse's house to anoint a new king, He did not tell him who the king would be. Samuel obeyed God and went because he believed God would speak to him when he arrived. His faith motivated his obedience, and his obedience completed his faith.

We see faith and obedience working together when Jesus instructed His disciples to . . .

> "Go to the village ahead of you, and just as you enter it, you will find a colt tied there, which no one has ever ridden. Untie it and bring it here. If anyone asks you, 'Why are you doing this?' tell him, 'The Lord needs it and will send it back here shortly.'"
>
> MARK 11:2,3

For the two disciples to complete this task, they had to take their commitment to obedience seriously. Maybe they played out different scenarios in their minds of all the bad things that could happen to them. (This would be like walking into a man's garage and driving away with his Lexus!) Or maybe they had seen Jesus provide for them so many times that they were assured this would turn out just like He said it would.

> They went and found a colt outside in the street, tied at a doorway. As they untied it, some people standing there asked, "What are you doing, untying that colt?" They answered as Jesus had told them to, and the people let them go.
>
> MARK 11:4-6

Faith should express itself in obedience. Faith that does not express itself in obedience is not Bible faith at all.

Faith is acting on the Word.

Real faith is expressed by acting on the Word.

> In the same way, faith by itself, if it is not accompanied by action, is dead. But someone will say, "You have faith; I have deeds." Show me your faith without

78

deeds, and I will show you my faith by my deeds. . . . As the body without the spirit is dead, so faith without deeds is dead.

JAMES 2:17,18,26

The obvious implication from this verse is that you cannot show a person your faith in any other way than by your actions. Therefore, if a person has no actions, he has no faith.

James continues his explanation of the relationship between faith and works by providing evidence that actions are the expression of faith. He reminds us that Abraham, because of his faith in God, offered up his son Isaac on the altar. His actions complemented his faith and made his faith complete.

"The doer is he who from the heart embraces God's word and *testifies by his life* that he really believes, according to the saying of Christ, 'Blessed are they who hear God's word and keep it.'"[7]

William Carey was burdened as a young man by the desire to take the Gospel to the world. The vast majority of church leaders, however, did not share his zeal. When he proposed to a meeting of ministers:

". . . the command given to the apostles to teach all nations was binding on all succeeding ministers to the end of the world . . ."

He was greeted with this response:

---

[7] Calvin's Commentary *on James 1:22-27.*

"Young man sit down! When God pleases to convert the heathen, he'll do it without consulting you or me!"

But God was not converting the heathen without them. Carey was convinced that faith in the Great Commission should be expressed by the obedient action of going. So in 1793, with the backing of the mission society he established, he took it upon himself to obey the Great Commission and went to India.

The expected lifespan of an Englishman in rural India in the late 1700s was six months. But in spite of the humid, unsanitary conditions, Carey survived malaria, dysentery, cholera, tigers, and cobras, and ministered for forty-one years without a furlough. He preached for seven years before he baptized his first convert! Through intense hardships, his indefatigable spirit and strong confidence in God's call carried him through to victory. His often repeated motto was, "Expect great things from God; attempt great things for God."

Conclusion

In this chapter, we have seen that faith is a relationship with God, total trust in His character, complete confidence in His written Word, obedience to God, and acting on the Word. In the next chapter, we will examine four more definitions of faith.

APPLICATION

Discuss

1. Which of the characteristics of faith in this chapter is the easiest for you to believe? Which is the most difficult? Has this changed since you first came into a relationship with God?

_____

_____

_____

2. Why do you think approaching faith as a formula is easier? Have you ever found yourself looking at faith as a formula rather than a relationship? If yes, why? What can you do to ensure that you will not fall into that trap again?

_____

_____

_____

3. Unbelief shows up in so many ways in our lives: worry, fear, doubt, anxiety. Why are all these forms of unbelief such an insult to God? What does it say about His character?

_____

_____

_____

4. Because faith is an action, it is revealed in how we respond when we receive bad news. Think back to the last time you received bad news. How did you respond? How should you have responded? What can you do to ensure that the next time you hear bad news, you will respond in faith?

Act

Read Hebrews 11 and record your insights concerning what faith is.

Memorize

Now faith is the assurance of things hoped for, the conviction of things not seen.

HEBREWS 11:1 (NASB)

CHAPTER 6

What is Faith?
Part 3

In the last chapter, we began our examination of what faith is. We concluded that faith is:

- A relationship with God
- Total trust in God's character
- Complete confidence in God's written Word
- Obedience to God
- Acting on the Word

In this chapter, we will continue to look at what faith is.

Faith is agreeing with God's Word even when it is contrary to circumstances.

Paul gives us a graphic description of the faith of our father Abraham.

> Without weakening in his faith, he faced the fact that his body was as good as dead—since he was about a hundred years old—and that Sarah's womb was also dead. Yet he did not waver through unbelief regarding the promise of God, but was strengthened in his faith and gave glory to God, being fully persuaded that God had power to do what he had promised.
>
> ROMANS 4:19-21

Abraham's faith was not an uninformed faith; it was not a faith divorced from reality. He contemplated his own body. He faced the facts. He recognized how old he was. He knew how dead Sarah's womb was. He was aware, very aware, of the odds against him having a child, and he weighed the facts carefully. But in the midst of all his careful analysis, he did not become weak in faith. In the end, the promise of God carried more weight than his circumstances—as hopeless as they seemed. As F.F. Bruce said:

> "Abraham did not shut his eyes to these unfavorable circumstances; he took them into careful consideration. But when he set them over against the promise of God, he found that the certainty of God's ability and will to fulfill His promise outweighed them all."[1]

In the late 1990s, I led a discipleship training program for the ministry organization that employed me. One particular year, the Lord directed me to believe for nineteen students. I then began the process of praying and declaring my faith. Three weeks prior to the start of the nine-month program, I had the desired nineteen students. But just before class began, I received a call from one student telling me he would not be able to attend. So I began the year with eighteen students. But I had prayed for nineteen, and I continued to believe God that I would have nineteen—even though it was contrary to my circumstances.

If someone would have asked me in the first weeks of the program, "How many students do you have?", I would have replied, "Eighteen," because that was how many I had, and I am a faith realist. I don't say things that aren't true.

---

[1] Tyndale New Testament Commentaries: Romans, *109,110.*

The King James Version and the New King James Version are the only major Bible versions that translate Romans 4:19 "he considered <u>not</u> his own body." The KJV is based on the manuscript called the Textus Receptus, *compiled by Desiderius Erasmus at the beginning of the sixteenth century. Erasmus's work was a huge accomplishment for the times, especially considering the scarcity of manuscripts that were available. However, an explosion of discoveries and linguistic research in the nineteenth and twentieth centuries rendered the* Textus Receptus *relatively obsolete.*

The English word "not" used in the KJV is translated from a simple Greek particle of negation. All of the better manuscripts do not have this particle. That is why all the versions of the last century translate Romans 4:19 something like "Abraham contemplated his own body."

It is very possible at this point to be confused about the message of faith. People often make outlandish claims and statements that do not reflect the facts, and all the time thinking that is what faith is. But we should learn a lesson from Abraham—the ultimate faith realist. He did not ignore the truth of his physical condition. He looked the facts squarely in the eyes. But he showed greater respect for God's promise and agreed with God's Word even when it was contrary to his circumstances. He put God's Word first, and when he did, his faith grew stronger—even as the situation grew more impossible.

After a few weeks of class, a pastor called and asked if one of his members could come sit in the class for a few days and see if it was the right thing for him to do. I said it was fine, and after the first day the young man told me he thought God wanted him to join the class. I told him I was sure God wanted him to—he was number nineteen.

Faith does not deny reality, it just acknowledges that there is something more real: the Word of God. This is not always easy, especially when our natural reason and our five physical senses are being bombarded with contrary circumstances. But it is how faith works. As Martin Luther said:

> "It is a quality of faith, that it wrings the neck of reason and strangles the beast, which else the whole world, with all creatures, could not strangle. But how? It holds to God's Word, and lets it be right and true, no matter how foolish and impossible it sounds. So did Abraham take his reason captive and slay it, inasmuch as he believed God's Word, wherein was promised him that from his unfruitful and as it were dead wife, Sarah, God would give him seed."[2]

Faith is seeing the unseen.

People commonly use the expression, "Seeing is believing."[3] The phrase usually refers to a person with a skeptical point of view, someone who requires tangible evidence before he will believe. I know something about this attitude. My home state is Missouri, commonly called the "Show-Me State." In 1899, Missouri congressman Willard Vandiver popularized the phrase when he said in a speech, "I come from a state that raises corn and cotton and cockleburs and Democrats, and frothy eloquence neither convinces nor satisfies me. I am from Missouri. You have got to show me."[4]

Jesus' disciple Thomas knew something about this attitude also—and it got him in a lot of trouble. His first mistake was to

---

[2] Martin Luther, Quoted in Philip Schaff, History of the Christian Church, *Volume VII, Chapter 1*.
[3] *The humorist James Thurber once said, "Seeing is deceiving." That may be a more accurate idiom.*
[4] Official Manual of the State of Missouri, *1979-1980, 1486*.

miss the evening meeting on Resurrection Sunday (John 20:24). We don't know why Thomas wasn't there—perhaps he had a prior engagement, an urgent errand, or maybe he was just worn out from all the recent activity.

But I am certain he regretted it later because the meeting turned out to be hugely important. It started when Jesus walked through the locked door—an impressive way to start any meeting! Jesus showed the disciples His pierced hands and His wounded side. Then He breathed on them and said, *"As the Father has sent me, I am sending you. . . . Receive the Holy Spirit. If you forgive anyone's sins, their sins are forgiven . . ."* (John 20:19-23).

When the other disciples saw Thomas later, they told him, *"We have seen the Lord!"*

But Thomas was unconvinced. He said, *"Unless I see the nail marks in his hands and put my finger where the nails were, and put my hand into his side, I will not believe."* He wanted evidence, tangible proof. He wanted to see it before he would believe it. (Thomas would have made a good Missourian.)

A week later, Thomas got his chance. He must have known he was in trouble when Jesus walked through the locked door again. *"Put your finger here . . ."* Jesus said. *"Stop doubting and believe."*

Thomas was smitten. All he could say was, *"My Lord and my God!"*

Jesus responded, *"Because you have seen me, you have believed; blessed are those who have not seen and yet have believed"* (John 20:27-29). Faith is not moved by what natural sight reveals.

Now faith is confidence in what we hope for and assurance about what we *do not see*.

HEBREWS 11:1

Faith sees something that the natural eyes cannot see.

By faith he [Moses] left Egypt, not fearing the king's
anger; he persevered because *he saw him who is
invisible*.

HEBREWS 11:27

Seeing is not believing in the traditional sense of the phrase
and the way Thomas understood it. But seeing is believing when
you see through the eyes of faith. This theme is everywhere in
the book of Hebrews.

By faith Moses . . . regarded disgrace for the sake of
Christ as of greater value than the treasures of Egypt,
because he was *looking* ahead to his reward.

HEBREWS 11:24,26

. . . In putting everything under them, God left nothing that is not subject to them. Yet at present we do
not see everything subject to them. But we do see
Jesus, who was made lower than the angels for a
little while, now crowned with glory and honor because he suffered death, so that by the grace of God
he might taste death for everyone.

HEBREWS 2:8,9

All these people were still living by faith when they died. They did not receive the things promised; they *only saw them* and welcomed them from a distance, admitting that they were foreigners and strangers on earth.

HEBREW 11:13

. . . fixing our eyes on Jesus . . . For the joy set before him he endured the cross, scorning its shame, and sat down at the right hand of the throne of God.

HEBREWS 12:2

So, "Seeing is believing"—when you are seeing what is unseen.

So we fix our eyes not on what is seen, but on what is unseen, since what is seen is temporary, but what is unseen is eternal.

2 CORINTHIANS 4:18

What is seen with our natural senses is temporary, fleeting, momentary—lasting only for a short time. It is subject to change, and *will* change in this transient world. But what is unseen (by our natural senses, perhaps, but perceived by the eye of faith) is eternal, unchanging, permanent—lasting forever. For heaven and earth will pass away, but God's Word stands forever. Augustine said:

"Faith is to believe what you do not see; the reward of this faith is to see what you believe."

Several years ago, we had a recent college graduate living in our home. David was on his way to the University of Arkansas as a full-time campus minister. But he had a problem: he did not own a car. If he was going to have a chance to be successful in campus ministry, he was going to need reliable transportation.

While David was reading the testimony of the Korean pastor Dr. Yonggi Cho, he was struck by how the Lord taught Cho the importance of praying specific prayers. Cho needed transportation for his ministry to the poor and needy in Seoul, and so he asked the Lord for a bicycle. He prayed in faith, but after six months, he still did not have a bicycle. When he spoke to the Lord about it, the Lord said, "I do not know what kind of bicycle you want." Cho then described to the Lord a precise picture of the bicycle he wanted, and in a short time he had it.

God stirred David's heart at that moment to believe for the car he needed. He decided (after careful deliberation) to ask for a powder blue, Volkswagen Rabbit with a diesel engine (gasoline had reached the unimaginable price of $1.38 per gallon and this car got 55 miles per gallon). He also wanted a high-end Blaupunkt stereo system. Searching through several magazines, David found a picture of the car he wanted and hung it on his wall. Every day he would look at the picture, meditate on the promises of God, and thank God for his powder blue, Volkswagen Rabbit diesel with a Blaupunkt stereo.

A few months later, I received a call from a minister friend who had heard David was in need of a car. He said, "A member of my church has a car he wants to give to someone starting out in ministry, and he wondered if David was the person he should give it to."

I said, "That depends. What kind of car is it?"

"It is a Volkswagen Rabbit," he replied.

"Is it a diesel?" I asked.

After a moment's hesitation he said, "Yes, I think it is."

"What color is it?"

"Light blue," he said.

"Could you call that powder blue?"

"Yes, I suppose you could," replied my friend. He continued, "And he just installed a very expensive German stereo that I think is called Blaupunkt or something like that."

"David will take the car!"

And he did! David saw the unseen, and it became more real to him than the physical world.[5] As Dr. J. Oswald Sanders said:

> "Faith enables the believing soul to treat the future as present and the invisible as seen."[6]

Faith is giving a good report.

> Then Caleb silenced the people before Moses and said, "We should go up and take possession of the land, for we can certainly do it." But the men who had gone up with him said, "We can't attack those people; they are stronger than we are." And they spread among the Israelites a bad report about the land they had explored. They said, "The land we explored devours those living in it. All the people we saw there are of great size."
>
> NUMBERS 13:30-32

---

[5] *This story is not a license to claim any kind of car or other material possession and start visualizing its existence. It is easy to become excessive at this point and start claiming anything you want. David clearly needed a car to obey God's will, and he prayed in line with God's purpose and not his own. The point of the story is simply that by faith we will often see the answer before we receive it.*

[6] *Quoted in Warren Wiersbe, Be Confident, 122.*

Twelve men went to spy out the land. They all had the same assignment: spy out the land and determine the best strategy for taking it. However, when they were going to report their findings, two distinct groups emerged. One group of ten saw the impossibility of the circumstances and gave a bad report: *"We can't attack those people; they are stronger than we are."* The other group of two saw the power and promises of God and gave a good report: *"We should go up and take possession of the land, for we can certainly do it."*

The first group was telling the truth: there were real giants in the land. But they could not see beyond the obstacles in their way, and so their report was filled with doubt and fear. The second group was also telling the truth: God was a lot bigger than any giant, and so were His covenant promises. They could see beyond the obstacles in their way, and so their report was filled with faith and courage.

Both groups saw the same things, but they processed what they saw through an entirely different filter. The people who gave the bad report saw only the physical reality in front of them. The people who gave the good report saw the same physical reality, but through the filter of God's Word.

A good report, then, is a faith-filled declaration of God's perspective of reality.

I read a story years ago that provides a natural example of what a good report looks like. It concerns the American war hero Lieutenant General Lewis "Chesty" Puller. Puller was the most decorated Marine in history with over fifty-two medals.[7] Even though he retired from active duty in 1955 and died in 1971, it is still a common occurrence for Marines in

---

[7] *He collected five Navy Crosses, three Air Medals, two Legion of Merits, a Distinguished Service Cross, Silver Star, Bronze Star, and Purple Heart, just to name a few.*

boot camp to end the day with the incantation, "Good night, Chesty Puller, wherever you are!"

Puller's confidence in battle was a constant encouragement to his men. One time, when his aggressive tactics had caused the enemy to completely surround his unit, he uttered the words he is most well known for, "They're on our left, they're on our right, they're in front of us, they're behind us . . . they can't get away this time!"

That is the ultimate good report!

Faith is a decision that never wavers.

James gives us a vivid metaphor of the instability of unbelief.

> But when you ask, you must believe and not doubt, because the one who doubts is like a wave of the sea, blown and tossed by the wind. That person should not expect to receive anything from the Lord. Such a person is double-minded and unstable in all they do.
>
> JAMES 1:6-8

The Greek word translated "doubt" in this passage presents a picture of a mind at war and divided against itself. Here is what three different commentators said about this passage:

> "The man who is not thoroughly persuaded . . . resembles a wave of the sea; he is in a state of continual agitation; driven by the wind, and tossed: now rising by hope, then sinking by despair."[8]

---

[8] Adam Clarke's Commentary.

"The wave of the sea has no stability. It is at the mercy of every wind, and seems to be driven and tossed every way. So he that comes to God with unsettled convictions, is liable to be driven about by every new feeling that may spring up in the mind. At one moment, hope and faith impel him to come to God; then the mind is at once filled with uncertainty and doubt, and the soul is as agitated and restless as the ocean."[9]

"The man who asks without faith is a walking contradiction. His answer will only be as firm as his request. James coined a new expression, 'double minded,' to describe this kind of man. He speaks of someone who maintains two entirely opposite mind-sets at the same time—first operating from one, then the other."[10]

There are many promises in God's Word, but this is not one you want to claim: *That person should not expect to receive anything from the Lord.* This is not just a warning and a rebuke but it is also a promise—not the kind of promise we might see embroidered on a tapestry or ornately lettered on a poster—but a promise nonetheless. And God is always faithful to keep His promises. If you waver and doubt, you will receive nothing from the Lord.[11]

---

[9] Barnes' Notes.

[10] New Commentary on the Whole Bible.

[11] *God is sovereign, and He does what He pleases at all times. Sometimes that means doing something when our faith is weak or nonexistent. This fact does not disprove this verse. It only means that the general rule is that God has chosen to respond to faith and that He expects us to believe and not to waver.*

A double-minded man is one who will not make a quality decision. He is John Bunyan's character "Mr. Facing-both-ways" from *Pilgrim's Progress*. He is the man with two brains. He is unstable and fickle, staggering and reeling like a drunken man. And he is always looking for reasons life has not worked out for him the way he planned.

The converse is true for a man who holds steadfast to God's Word without wavering.

"If we find a man who takes hold of the promises of God with firmness; who feels the deepest assurance when he prays that God will hear prayer; who always goes to Him without hesitation in his perplexities and trials, never wavering, we shall find one who is firm in his principles, steady in his integrity, settled in his determinations, and steadfast in his plans of life."[12]

Surely the righteous will never be shaken; they will be remembered forever. They will have no fear of bad news; their hearts are steadfast, trusting in the LORD. Their hearts are secure, they will have no fear; in the end they will look in triumph on their foes.

PSALM 112:6-8

The man who looks in triumph on his foes is a man who made a quality decision. A quality decision is one that you do not go back on; it's the opposite of a New Year's Resolution.

I overheard two trainers talking a few years ago at the health club I frequented. One had been there a long time and the other

---

[12] Barnes' Notes.

was fairly new. The new trainer said, "The club has been very crowded the last week." (It was early January.) The other trainer who had seen this many times replied, "Just wait a few weeks and they will all be gone!"

And they were! Because they had never made a quality decision. When the challenge of change became too great, they opted for the easy way out. But that is not what Bible faith is. Bible faith begins with a quality decision to put the Word of God first, and it never looks back.

Luke presented an example of a quality decision from the life of Jesus:

> As the time approached for him to be taken up to heaven, Jesus resolutely set out for Jerusalem.
>
> LUKE 9:51

The dictionary defines "resolute" as "firm and unwavering; characterized by determination and purpose; unyielding, steadfast, and tenacious." Jesus made a quality decision to resolutely head toward Jerusalem—even though He knew what was waiting for Him there. And because we are new creations in Christ, we have the same ability to make quality decisions— not by might or by power, but by His Spirit. This is not human willpower. It is the Spirit of Him who raised Jesus from the dead living in us—giving life to our mortal bodies (Romans 8:11). It is the grace of God teaching us *to live self-controlled, upright and godly lives in this present age* (Titus 2:11-14). It is the resurrection power of Jesus enabling us to live a new life (Romans 6:3-7).

Conclusion

In these chapters, we have examined the foundation of faith, why we need it, and what it is. In the following chapters, we will look at how faith grows.

APPLICATION

Discuss

1. What was so remarkable about Abraham's faith as described by Paul in Romans 4:19-21? Why do you think that an informed and realistic faith is difficult for people to understand? Have you encountered the challenge of having to face facts squarely in the eye without losing faith? What did God teach you in those circumstances?

   _____

   _____

   _____

2. Why is the attitude of Thomas common among believers? When was the last time you displayed Thomas-like behavior when you were faced with a situation that required Abraham-like faith? Why did you find it difficult to make the right response? What did you learn from that experience that will help you the next time you encounter something similar?

   _____

   _____

   _____

3. Some people find it harder than others to give a good report, maybe because of their upbringing or their temperament or other factors, but they have a natural tendency to negativity. What is your tendency when faced with potent-

ially negative circumstances? Are you more prone to a bad report? If so, why, and what can you do about it?

_____

_____

_____

4. People of faith make quality decisions based on the Word of God. What situation are you facing right now that requires a quality decision? What are the obstacles hindering you from making the decision, and how will you overcome them?

_____

_____

_____

Act

Review the last three chapters on what faith is. Examine the current state of your faith and create an action plan to immediately begin to maximize the areas that you are strong in and improve the areas that you are weak in.

Memorize

But when you ask, you must believe and not doubt, because the one who doubts is like a wave of the sea, blown and tossed by the wind. That person should not expect to receive anything from the Lord. Such a person is double-minded and unstable in all they do.

JAMES 1:6-8

CHAPTER 7

How does Faith Grow?
Part 1

N early everyone is conscious of our need for more faith. Meeting someone who would say "I have too much faith" is highly unlikely. Such people, if they exist at all, are extremely rare. Most people would say the opposite—"I do not have enough faith." So then, where do we get more faith? There are a number of answers to that question, but the starting point is this simple fact: if you are a Christian, you already have faith. Paul said to the Romans:

> . . . God has allotted to each a measure of faith.
>
> ROMANS 12:3 (NASB)

God has given to each of us a measure or portion of faith. Think of it as our *Faith Starter Kit*. Everything we need to get started is already in the package. But there are some things we have to add to the *Kit* to make our faith grow. Think of these as *Faith Additives*. The dictionary defines the word "additive" as something added to something else to improve or strengthen it.

So God gives us faith, and then, by His grace, we add to it. This causes our faith to grow. Simple enough? Then let's look at five *Faith Additives* for growing strong faith.

Faith grows by hearing the Word of God.

The clearest answer to the question how faith grows is found in Paul's letter to the Romans.

> Consequently, faith comes from hearing the message, and the message is heard through the word about Christ.
>
> ROMANS 10:17

This familiar verse should not be lifted out of the chapter without any reference to its setting. The context of the verse is preaching, and the apostle emphasizes in the verses before and after this verse that it is the *preached Word* that produces faith in the hearer. Our private devotional interaction with the Word of God is certainly important and it does increase our faith, but hearing the Word preached under the anointing is the best and fastest way to cause our faith to grow. There is a good example of this in Luke's account of an incident that took place during Paul's preaching ministry in Lystra.

> . . . where they continued to preach the gospel. In Lystra there sat a man who was lame. He had been that way from birth and had never walked. He listened to Paul as he was speaking. Paul looked directly at him, saw that he had faith to be healed and called out, "Stand up on your feet!" At that, the man jumped up and began to walk.
>
> ACTS 14:7-10

Luke tells us that Paul saw that this man had the faith needed to be healed. Where did this man get the faith? God gave it to him as he heard the Word that Paul preached under the anointing. This is a clear example of the principle in Romans 10:17: faith comes by hearing the Word of God preached. In the same way, faith will come to us as we steadfastly listen to the preached Word.

Because faith comes from hearing God's Word, the best way to increase our faith is to increase the amount of time we spend listening to it. Martin Luther said:

> "God creates faith in us through the Word. He increases, strengthens, and confirms faith in us through His Word. Therefore, the best service that anybody can render God is diligently to hear and read God's Word."[1]

But does hearing God's Word *automatically* increase our faith? Is it possible to hear God's Word without our faith growing at all? The writer of Hebrews says that this is possible when he reminds us of the Israelites who fell in the wilderness even after they listened to God's Word. They heard the Word, but their faith did not increase.

> For we also have had the gospel preached to us, just as they did; but the message they heard was of no value to them, because those who heard did not combine it with faith.
>
> HEBREWS 4:2 (NASB)

The Greek word translated "combine" in this passage is *kerannumi*, which means, "a mixing of two things, so that they are blended and form a new compound." There is a similar but different Greek word used in other places in the Scriptures

---

[1] Commentary on Paul's Epistle to the Galatians.

for "combine." It is *mignumi*, which implies "a mixing together without such composition."

An experiment I did in high school chemistry class will help us understand the difference between the two words. The teacher started the experiment with a quantity of sodium, an element so highly reactive it explodes on contact with water. Then she added the poisonous gas chlorine. After combining these two dangerous elements together, she was able to eat the product. It was common table salt. This is what the word *kerannumi* means—mixing two things together to get something new.

However, *mignumi* is comparable to combining oil and vinegar in a container. If we shake the container vigorously, the two compounds will not form anything new. They may seem to combine briefly, but they will still retain their original characteristics. Before long, the oil will settle at the bottom and the vinegar on top.

This describes what the Israelites did. They heard the Word of God, but they never allowed it to do anything in their hearts. They did not combine it *(kerannumi)* with a decision to believe. They heard the Word, but they retained their original characteristics *(mignumi)*, and they were not transformed and changed.

So then, hearing is not enough—we must actively decide to believe the words we are hearing. Paul calls this "hearing with faith."

I would like to learn just one thing from you: Did you receive the Spirit by the works of the law, or by *believing what you heard*? . . . So again I ask, does God give you his Spirit and work miracles among you by the works of the law, or by your *believing what you heard*?

GALATIANS 3:2,5

I once prayed with a college student who was distraught because she could not receive the Holy Spirit and speak in tongues. She told me, "I cannot speak in tongues. I do not know what my problem is. I try and try, but for some reason I cannot speak in tongues. I have had prayer several times, but I cannot speak in tongues!"

After she calmed down a bit I said to her, "I can tell you what your problem is."

She looked at me, and a glimmer of hope appeared on her countenance. "You can?" she said meekly.

I said, "You have just told me what you believe. You expressed what you really believe with the words you said. Three times you said, 'I cannot speak in tongues.' Now, let me ask you this question, what does the Bible say will happen when I lay my hands upon you?"

"I will be filled with the Holy Spirit and speak with tongues," she said.

"I am sorry," I said, "I did not hear you. Would you repeat that please?"

"I will be filled with the Holy Spirit and speak with tongues," she said a little louder.

"I am sorry, there must be something wrong with my hearing; could you say that again?"

"I will be filled with the Holy Spirit and speak with tongues," she said with greater force.

I said, "All you have done so far is undo the three negative faith declarations you made earlier. Now," I said, "tell me what you believe."

"I will be filled with the Holy Spirit and speak with tongues."

I then called three of her girlfriends over and made her say it four times to them. By then she was ready. We laid our hands on her, she received the Holy Spirit, and spoke in tongues fluently.

She had heard the Word concerning the infilling of the Holy Spirit many times, but it had been of no value to her. But when she "heard with faith"—when she made a quality decision to believe what she heard—she received immediately.

The Israelites referred to in Hebrews 4:2 heard the Word of God but would not believe. The writer of the letter describes their unbelief and disobedience in great detail in this section as a warning to us. There is much we do not know about the letter to the Hebrews, but one thing we are sure of is that the recipients were a congregation in danger of drifting away from faith in Christ. The author continually exhorts them concerning the danger of unbelief.

> So, as the Holy Spirit says: "Today, if you hear his voice, do not harden your hearts as you did in the rebellion, during the time of testing in the wilderness, where your ancestors tested and tried me, though for forty years they saw what I did. . . ." See to it, brothers and sisters, that none of you has a sinful, unbelieving heart that turns away from the living God.
>
> HEBREWS 3:7-9,12

Unbelief is called sinful in this passage. The author continues:

> And with whom was he *angry* for forty years? Was it not with those who sinned, whose bodies perished in the wilderness?
>
> HEBREWS 3:17

Apparently, unbelief makes God angry. This is confirmed by an incident recorded by Mark concerning the unbelief of Jesus' disciples after His resurrection.

> When Jesus rose early on the first day of the week, he appeared first to Mary Magdalene, out of whom he had driven seven demons. She went and told those who had been with him and who were mourning and weeping. When they heard that Jesus was alive and that she had seen him, they did not believe it. Afterward Jesus appeared in a different form to two of them while they were walking in the country. These returned and reported it to the rest; but they did not believe them either. Later Jesus appeared to the Eleven as they were eating; he *rebuked* them for their lack of faith and their *stubborn refusal to believe* those who had seen him after he had risen.
>
> Mark 16:9-14

The Greek word translated "rebuked" in this passage is a very strong word meaning "to reprimand or criticize angrily, vehemently, and at length." The only other time this word was used in reference to Jesus was when He denounced the cities of Korazin and Capernaum because they did not repent after seeing His miracles (Matthew 11:20). Jesus was especially angry at His disciples on this occasion because of their *stubborn refusal to believe*. It was not just an intellectual problem or a lack of information behind their unbelief; it was a choice not to believe.

Continuing in Hebrews . . .

> And to whom did God swear that they would never enter his rest if not to those who disobeyed? So we see that they were not able to enter, because of their unbelief.
>
> Hebrews 3:18,19

Disobedience and unbelief are coupled in this pair of verses as synonyms, as two expressions of the same act. Unbelief is disobedience and disobedience is unbelief. The warnings continue into the next chapter:

> Therefore, since the promise of entering his rest still stands, let us be careful that none of you be found to have fallen short of it.
>
> Hebrews 4:1

The author then compares the life of faith with the Sabbath rest promised to God's people—a rest from our own works in imitation of God and how He rested from His works after the creation of the world. He concludes this section with an exhortation to make every effort to enter that rest, so that no one will fall short by following their example of disobedience. The emphasis of this entire passage is "hearing His voice."

- If you hear His voice, you will enter the Sabbath rest.
- If you hear His voice, you will not fall through unbelief.
- If you hear His voice, you will not be disobedient.
- If you hear His voice, you will have faith to endure.

After saying all this, he tells them how they can be sure to hear His voice.

For the word of God is alive and active. . . .

HEBREWS 4:12

God's voice is His Word, and if we hear it by faith, faith will increase.

Faith grows by meditating on the Word of God.

The psalmist uses the metaphor of a tree to paint an attractive picture of the man who delights in meditating on God's Word.

> . . . but whose delight is in the law of the LORD, and who meditates on his law day and night. That person is like a tree planted by streams of water, which yields its fruit in season and whose leaf does not wither—whatever they do prospers.
>
> PSALM 1:2,3

The following are a few thoughts concerning this passage.

- Albert Barnes, in his *Commentary on the Psalms*, said about this man, "He disciplines his mind to meditate habitually and intentionally. He does this at set times each day and during the brief moments of leisure and down-time of every day."[2] Meditation is not just a part of our daily devotional time. It is something we engage in all throughout our day.
- This tree is planted; it did not just grow at random. And because it was planted, there must have been a "planter," someone who put the tree exactly where it is for a

---

[2] *Inspired by* Barnes' Notes, *comment on Psalm 1:2.*

specific purpose. God has planted us where we are for His divine purpose.

- The tree is not just planted, it is planted firmly. A firmly planted tree is one with an extensive root system. There is a hidden world underground that supports the tree against the elements of the world. Come what will, this tree will still be standing. This same idea is captured in Psalm 112:

> . . . Blessed are those who fear the LORD, who find great delight in his commands. . . . Surely the righteous will never be shaken; they will be remembered forever. They will have no fear of bad news; their hearts are steadfast, trusting in the LORD. Their hearts are secure, they will have no fear; in the end they will look in triumph on their foes.
>
> PSALM 112:1,6-8

- The tree is planted firmly by streams of water. Notice that the word "streams" is plural. There is more than one so that if one should fail, there are others to depend on.[3] This is a reference to the complex irrigation system used in the Middle East—a system that made parts of Egypt the most fertile and productive ground in the world. Rivers were redirected so that dozens of streams would flow in canals on the cultivated land. This produced a constant and abundant flow of life-giving water to ensure fruitfulness regardless of weather conditions. The person who meditates constantly on God's

---

[3] *Inspired by Charles Spurgeon,* The Treasury of David, *comment on Psalm 1:3.*

Word does *not fear when the heat comes*; he *will not be anxious in a year of drought nor cease to yield fruit* (Jeremiah 17:8 NASB).

- Because of this endless supply of life-giving water, the tree is always green and it always yields fruit.

The last phrase of the verse, *whatever they do prospers,* is a summary of all the above qualities. Note that there are no qualifiers connected with this phrase. The author does not say, "Whatever they do prospers, *if* it is the will of God," or, "Whatever they do prospers, *if* their motives are right." He simply states that whatever they do will prosper.

Why are there no qualifiers in this verse? Can we do anything we want—regardless if it is the will of God or not—and expect it to prosper? Certainly not. But the reason there are no qualifiers in this verse is because a man meditating on God's Word day and night will walk naturally in God's will. God's Word *is* His will, and if we constantly meditate on His Word, we will naturally walk in His will. This is because meditation produces obedience.

> "Keep this Book of the Law always on your lips; meditate on it day and night, *so* that you may be careful to do everything written in it. Then you will be prosperous and successful."
>
> JOSHUA 1:8

The word "so" in this verse indicates cause and effect. Because you meditate on the Word of God day and night, you *will* be careful to obey it.

When God said to Abraham, *"I will surely bless you and make your descendants as numerous as the stars in the sky and as the sand on the seashore. Your descendants will take possession of the cities of their enemies"* (Genesis 22:17), He was giving him something to meditate on during the day (sand), and something to meditate on during the night (stars).

James communicated the same idea when he said:

> But whoever looks intently into the perfect law that gives freedom, and continues in it—not forgetting what they have heard, but doing it—they will be blessed in what they do.
>
> JAMES 1:25

Looking intently at the Word of God is meditating on it. If we practice this, we will be blessed in what we do.

Faith grows by patience.

Paul described Abraham's faith this way:

> . . . yet, with respect to the promise of God, he did not waver in unbelief, but grew strong in faith, giving glory to God . . .
>
> ROMANS 4:20 (NASB)

Abraham *grew* strong in faith. He did not necessarily start out strong in faith. If you read his story in Genesis, you know that is true. On a number of occasions, he acted in unbelief and sought to make things happen through his own efforts. But gradually his faith grew, and eventually he inherited God's promises.

112

Faith grows when we give it time to grow. Not everything happens overnight in God's kingdom. Not all results come immediately. Not all miracles are instantaneous. Instead, most of God's work is gradual. And because it is gradual, we must be patient.

When my oldest son was in pre-kindergarten Sunday school, his teacher brought seeds for the class to plant as an illustration of faith. Enthusiastically, he planted his seeds in the container provided by the teacher. The next Sunday, he could not wait for the family to get to church so he could see his plant. But when we arrived, we saw the seed had not grown. I encouraged him that the seed was like faith, and that it would grow if we gave it time and proper care. The next Sunday, he was dismayed when he saw everyone had a little plant growing in their container—but he had nothing.

Waiting for his seed to grow had been difficult, but *now* it was excruciating. What was wrong with his seed? Did he do something wrong? Did God not love him as much as the other children? All of these thoughts went through his young mind. It got so bad I did not want to go to church anymore! Finally, after four weeks, the seed sprouted and a little plant grew in his container. My son was happy and life was good again. Faith does grow, if it is given time and proper care.

Conclusion

If we are believers, we already have faith. However, that faith will not do us much good unless we add the right ingredients. We have already seen three important faith additives. In the next chapter, we will examine two more.

APPLICATION

Discuss

1. Why are there so many warnings about unbelief in the Bible? What area of unbelief are you dealing with right now? Why are you finding it so difficult to believe, and what can you do to change?

   _____

   _____

   _____

2. There is a difference between hearing God's Word actively and hearing God's Word passively. The first produces faith and the second produces nothing. Are you ever guilty of hearing God's Word passively? Why do you think that is? What can you do to ensure that every time you hear God's Word, you hear it with faith?

   _____

   _____

   _____

3. Constant meditation on God's Word produces faith, obedience, and success. But it is not always easy to do. What are some of the obstacles you face that hinder you from meditating on God's Word? What is one action step you can take immediately to start increasing the amount of time you spend meditating on God's Word?

_____

_____

_____

4. We inherit the promises through faith and patience. What specific promise from God are you waiting on at this time? What are the challenges you are facing as you wait? How can you encourage yourself to continue to hold onto God's promise while you wait?

_____

_____

_____

Act

Make a commitment to double the amount of time you spend in God's Word for one week. At the end of the week, evaluate the benefits you received from the exercise. Then create a method to incrementally increase your time in God's Word until you get it to the ideal place.

Memorize

Consequently, faith comes from hearing the message, and the message is heard through the word about Christ.

ROMANS 10:17

CHAPTER 8

How does Faith Grow?
Part 2

In the last chapter, we began our examination of how faith grows. We concluded that faith grows through . . .

- Hearing the Word of God
- Meditating on the Word of God
- Patience

In this chapter, we will continue to look at how faith grows.

Faith grows by speaking the Word of God.

There is a strong connection in Scripture between our faith and the words of our mouth. When the disciples asked Jesus to increase their faith, He told them, *"If you have faith . . . you can say . . ."* (Luke 17:5,6). The author of Hebrews urged the saints to endure difficult times by holding fast to the *confession of their faith* (Hebrews 4:14 NASB). Paul said the very spirit of faith was connected to the words of our mouth.

> It is written: "I believed; therefore I have spoken." Since we have that same spirit of faith, we also believe and therefore speak . . .
>
> 2 Corinthians 4:13

Paul also said that the very process through which we are saved displays the connection between faith and speaking.

> If you *declare* with your mouth, "Jesus is Lord," and *believe* in your heart that God raised him from the dead, you will be saved. For it is with your heart that you *believe* and are justified, and it is with your mouth that you *profess* your faith and are saved.
>
> ROMANS 10:9,10

Everywhere we look in Scripture, we see how important words are and how they affect our faith. Here are two reasons.

Reason #1: God created with words.

When the Bible opens in Genesis 1, we see God at work speaking the worlds into existence. The first time God is mentioned, He is speaking; this is the first revelation we have of Him. The phrase *God said* is repeated eleven times in the opening chapter.[1] Each time the phrase is used, something new is created. Everything God created, He created with words. Other verses confirm this fact:

> By the *word of the Lord* the heavens were made, their starry host by the *breath of his mouth*. . . . For he *spoke*, and it came to be; he *commanded*, and it stood firm.
>
> PSALM 33:6,9

> By faith we understand that the universe was formed at *God's command*, so that what is seen was not made out of what is visible.
>
> HEBREWS 11:3

---

[1] *Genesis 1:3,6,9,11,14,20,22,24,26,28,29.*

The Hebrew scholar Robert Alter said it this way:

> "In the biblical view, words underlie reality. God called the world into being with words. From the start, the capacity for using language set man apart from the other creatures. Spoken language, then, is the foundation of everything human and divine that transpires in the Bible."[2]

Another way the connection between God's creative acts and words is illustrated in the cursing of the fig tree—one of the most unusual incidents in the ministry of Jesus. Many of the commentators throughout history have understood the incident to be a censure of the spiritual state of the nation of Israel. The barren fig tree, they said, symbolically represented barren Israel[3] as reflected in their attitude toward the temple and the ministry of Jesus. These interpretations are certainly correct, but there is even more in this passage.

First of all, we must understand this incident as a teaching demonstration on the nature of faith. Jesus' own commentary when asked about the incident was, *"Have faith in God."* By saying this, He wanted His disciples to understand that it was an object lesson on the topic of what faith is and how it works. Jesus used two interconnected images to teach this lesson to His disciples: a barren fig tree and a barren nation. That is why the cleansing of the temple is sandwiched between the incident of the fig tree.

---

[2] *Robert Alter, The Art of Biblical Narrative, 69.*
[3] *In the following passages—Jeremiah 24:1-9, Hosea 9:10, and Luke 13:6-9—the connection between the imagery of the fig tree and the nation of Israel is clearly demonstrated.*

The story starts with a visit to the temple.

> Jesus entered Jerusalem and went into the temple courts. He looked around at everything, but since it was already late, he went out to Bethany with the Twelve.
>
> MARK 11:11

We are not told what Jesus was looking at in the temple or why He chose to visit it at this time—but possibly it was to plan His strategy for the next day.

> The next day as they were leaving Bethany, Jesus was hungry. Seeing in the distance a fig tree in leaf, he went to find out if it had any fruit. When he reached it, he found nothing but leaves, because it was not the season for figs. Then he said to the tree, "May no one ever eat fruit from you again." And his disciples heard him say it.
>
> MARK 11:12-14

This behavior may seem strange to us. If it was not the season for figs, why should Jesus expect figs? And if it was not the season for figs, why curse the poor tree for not bearing figs? A little botanical knowledge of Palestine will help us here. The noted scholar Ernest W. G. Masterman, writing in the *International Standard Bible Encyclopedia*, says:

> "When the young leaves are newly appearing in April, every fig-tree which is going to bear fruit at all will have some immature figs upon it, even though

'the time of figs,' (i.e. of ordinary edible figs) 'is not yet.' These immature figs are not only eaten today, but it is sure evidence that the tree bearing them is not barren."

Jesus knew it was not fig season, but He was not looking for figs. He was looking for the unripe figs about the size of small cherries that should have been on the tree. The fact that they were not was proof that the tree was barren and would not produce fruit at any season. And so Jesus spoke the inevitable result, *"May no one ever eat fruit from you again."* The disciples were listening, but they asked no questions. Perhaps Jesus did not appear ready to explain Himself at that time. He then proceeded to Jerusalem.

On reaching Jerusalem, Jesus entered the temple courts and began driving out those who were buying and selling there. He overturned the tables of the money changers and the benches of those selling doves, and would not allow anyone to carry merchandise through the temple courts. And as he taught them, he said, "Is it not written: 'My house will be called a house of prayer for all nations'? But you have made it 'a den of robbers.'" The chief priests and the teachers of the law heard this and began looking for a way to kill him, for they feared him, because the whole crowd was amazed at his teaching.

MARK 11:15-18

Israel had begun as a nation over 1800 years prior to this event. The nation's beginnings were rooted in Abraham, a man of great faith. Whenever Abraham is mentioned in the New Testament, it is nearly always in the context of his faith. He had many outstanding qualities, but his faith stands out above all of them.

But now Abraham's descendants have a barren faith, a faith that, like the fig tree, will produce no fruit. There should be fruit on the spiritual tree of Israel, but, just like the barren tree, there is none. The nation had already desecrated God's presence in the temple by making it a robbers' den, and they were about to desecrate God's presence in His Son by killing Him on a cross. They had destroyed the temple and were looking for ways to destroy Him. The story continues . . .

> When evening came, Jesus and his disciples went out of the city. In the morning, as they went along, they saw the fig tree withered from the roots. Peter remembered and said to Jesus, "Rabbi, look! The fig tree you cursed has withered!" "Have faith in God," Jesus answered.
>
> MARK 11:19-22

Jesus is famous for His non sequitors. A non sequitor is a statement that does not logically follow the statement that preceded it. For example, if I met you for the first time, I would introduce myself to you. If you responded to my introduction by saying, "It will rain on Tuesday," that would be a non sequitor. It may be a true statement, but it is out of sequence; it does not logically follow from my greeting. The statement, *"Have faith in God,"* appeared to be a non sequitor. It was not what the disciples expected to hear from Jesus because it did not logically follow the statement, *"The fig tree you cursed has withered."* You can almost hear Peter thinking, "Huh? I know we are supposed to have faith in God, but what does that have to do with the withered fig tree?"

But Peter did not realize that Jesus was not using a non sequitor; His statement did proceed logically from Peter's question. Peter was unaware that Jesus had contrived the whole scenario to create a memorable learning experience, one that neither Peter nor the other disciples would forget.

Jesus was saying to them, "Everything about the fig tree is a lesson on how faith works. I spoke, and it happened. That is how faith works, and that is the example I want you to follow. That is how I want you to have faith in God. Do not miss this lesson and end up like barren Israel." Jesus continues . . .

> "I tell you the truth, if anyone says to this mountain, 'Go, throw yourself into the sea,' and does not doubt in his heart but believes that what he says will happen, it will be done for him."
>
> MARK 11:23

Why did Jesus preface His comments with the phrase, *"I tell you the truth"*? Wasn't everything Jesus said the truth? Whenever anyone prefaces a comment to me with a similar statement, I want to ask them, "Haven't you been telling me the truth the whole time? Is there something I should question about what you have been telling me? Why do you feel the sudden need to emphasize that you are telling me the truth?" We know that Jesus always tells the truth. Why then did He need to make that introductory statement?

I think Jesus knew His next statements would be so staggering and so radically unexpected that He would need to reinforce them with the strongest language possible. If that is so, then what was so staggering about His next statements?

First, Jesus said, "If *anyone* says . . ." Jesus had just cursed the fig tree, and it had withered. That is a pretty astonishing feat. It would be easy to assume that only He could do something like that because, after all, He was the Son of God. But Jesus immediately corrected that kind of thinking when He used the word anyone. This is not just something that only the Son of God gets to do. *Anyone* can speak to the mountain. *Anyone* can have faith like that—from the greatest apostle to the youngest believer.

Second, Jesus said, ". . . to *this* mountain." His use of the definite article meant He was referring to (and possibly pointing to) a specific mountain. Why is this important? Because it means we cannot spiritualize His statement to mean only mountains in a metaphorical sense. Certainly there is a metaphorical application for mountains that is applicable to this passage (for example, mountains may be seen as problems, obstacles, demonic roadblocks, etc.), but it refers primarily to a physical reality. There is real power in our words, and Jesus used strong language to reinforce that truth.

Third, Jesus was very specific about what we have to believe. We have to believe that *what we say will come to pass.*

There are many things we have to believe about God. We have to believe that He is (Hebrews 11:6). We have to believe He sent His Son to die for us (John 3:16). We have to believe that He rose from the dead (Romans 10:9). But as important as those things are, they are not what Jesus said we have to believe in order to move mountains. We have to believe that *what we say will come to pass.* What an astonishing, mind-boggling truth. No wonder Jesus prefaced His statements with, *"I tell you the truth."*

The first time I heard this passage expounded on was in a sermon from an African minister who was visiting the United States. He recounted the time he first heard this truth as a Bible school student. After hearing the message, he decided he would put it in action. Outside his dorm room there was a small hill—no mountain, certainly, but a good place to start. He closed his eyes, pointed to the hill, and said confidently, "Hill, I command you to be taken up and cast into the sea; I do not doubt in my heart, but I believe that what I say is going to happen." He opened his eyes fully expecting the hill to be gone, but to his surprise and dismay, it was not.

Discouraged and confused, he finished the school term and left for summer break. He returned in the fall and was assigned his former room. Unpacking his clothes, he glanced out his window and saw that over the summer bulldozers had cleared the hill for new dormitories. He had commanded the hill to move, and it had—not how he imagined it would—but it was gone nonetheless.[4]

Reason #2: Words that are spoken in faith bring victory.

We all stumble in many ways. Anyone who is never at fault in what they say is perfect, able to keep their whole body in check. When we put bits into the mouths of horses to make them obey us, we can turn the whole animal. Or take ships as an example. Although they are so large and are driven by strong winds, they are steered by a very small rudder wherever the pilot wants to go.

JAMES 3:2-4

---

[4] I am not suggesting that this student's words moved the hill. The bulldozers did that. But God used this unique situation to teach him a valuable spiritual lesson, and to underscore just how powerful words can be.

James uses two pairs of metaphors in this passage: a horse and bridle, and a ship and rudder. Both pairs refer to the power of our words. Both pairs also carry the idea of destination: you ride on a horse to a particular location; you travel on a ship to another port. The idea we are supposed to understand from these metaphors is that our destination (or destiny) is closely connected with the words we speak.

In the first metaphor, James compares our words to the bridle of a horse. The bridle controls the direction of the horse. The metaphor is clear: words control our destiny the way the bridle controls the direction of the horse.

In the second metaphor, James repeats the meaning of the first and adds a few new ideas to it. He makes three statements about the ship:

- The ship is large.
- The ship is buffeted by strong winds.
- The rudder will hold the ship on course.

The application of this metaphor is also clear. The ship has a destination, and we have a destiny. The ship is large, and our destiny is significant. The ship is buffeted by strong winds, and opposing forces will try to knock us off our course. But through it all, the rudder will hold the ship on course. Our words, spoken in faith, are the rudder of our lives and they will keep us on course.[5]

---

[5] *Speaking God's Word is crucial to our faith development. There are a series of topical confessions for you to follow in Appendix C.*

Faith grows by acting on the Word of God.

> In the same way, faith by itself, if it is not accompanied by action, is dead. . . . Was not our father Abraham considered righteous for what he did when he offered his son Isaac on the altar? You see that his faith and his actions were working together, and his faith was made complete by what he did.
>
> JAMES 2:17,21,22

The Epistle of James deeply troubled Martin Luther because it appeared to teach justification by works. Early in his career, he even called it "an epistle of straw."[6] But he eventually understood that it was teaching an active faith, one that expressed itself in action.[7] He said:

> "Faith is a living, restless thing. It cannot be inoperative. We are not saved by works; but if there be no works, there must be something amiss with faith."[8]

James said that when Abraham acted on the Word of God, it completed or perfected his faith. The *New Commentary on the Whole Bible* says it this way:

> "His actions completed his faith—i.e., they manifested the full development and maturation of his faith. The seed has everything it needs to be a full-grown tree right from the start, but you can hardly

---

[6] *Quoted in the Preface of Martin Luther's 1522 German translation of the New Testament.*

[7] *In Luther's writings, he quoted over half of the 108 verses in James. He obviously believed it was the Word of God.*

[8] *Roland H. Bainton,* Here I Stand: A Life of Martin Luther *(New York: New American Library, 1950; 1978), 259.*

say it is complete until you see the towering tree. Good deeds show that our faith is full-grown at last."

A few other Bible translations underscore this point:

. . . the faith was working with his works, and out of the works the *faith was perfected*. (YLT)

You see that faith was active along with his works, and *faith was brought to completion* by the works. (NRSV)

Abraham's . . . *faith was made perfect* by what he did. (NCV)

His *faith was shown to be genuine* by what he did. (God's Word)

From these translations, we can clearly see that actions are integral to the growth of our faith.

I have a friend who struggled with a degenerative disc problem for years. She was always in pain, and nothing she did seemed to help. She had prayed and believed God for healing for a long time, but to no avail. Finally, in a time of desperation, she heard the Lord direct her to run a marathon. Nothing seemed more impossible. She could hardly walk, how would she ever run over twenty-six miles? But in obedience to God she put her faith in action. She trained for six months and, in January 2004, entered the Disney Marathon in Florida. She experienced pain throughout the race, but before crossing the finish line felt a "sudden twinge" and was completely healed. To this day, she has had no more problems.

She acted on the Word of the Lord and received a miracle. The cripple that Paul ministered to in Lystra had a similar experience.

> In Lystra there sat a man who was lame. He had been that way from birth and had never walked. He listened to Paul as he was speaking. Paul looked directly at him, saw that he had faith to be healed and called out, "Stand up on your feet!" At that, the man jumped up and began to walk.
>
> ACTS 14:8-10

It would have been easy for the lame man to explain to Paul that he would be glad to stand up on his feet—if God would only heal him first. But if he had said that instead of acting on his faith, he would not have been healed. His obedient and active response to the Word of truth caused his healing. His actions combined with his faith, and together they completed his healing.

An old Scotsman operated a rowboat for transporting passengers across one of the many lochs in his native land. Carved on one oar was the word, "Faith," and on the other oar the word, "Works." When a curious passenger asked him why, he responded with a demonstration. Using just the "Faith" oar, he rowed vigorously, but they just went in circles. Switching to the "Works" oar, he rowed again with the same results—but in the opposite direction. After the demonstration, he said, "In the Christian life, works without faith are as useless as faith without works: both of them will spin you in circles and get you nowhere. But together, in cooperation, they will take you anywhere you want to go."

Conclusion

In the last two chapters, we have examined how faith grows. In the next chapter, we will look at specific examples from God's Word of faith in action.

APPLICATION

Discuss

1. Many Christians seem to have a natural resistance to confessing God's Word with boldness and consistency. They start doing it, and then various obstacles arise until slowly they abandon the practice completely. Have you had a similar experience? If so, what are some of the obstacles that have deterred you? Why were those obstacles effective in deterring you, and what can you do to ensure they will not defeat you again?

    _____

    _____

    _____

2. Our destination in life is closely connected with the words we speak. What are some of the "spiritual destinations" you desire in your life, and what confessions should you make in order to get there? What creative action step can you take to incorporate more confession in your life?

    _____

    _____

    _____

3. Our actions reveal what we believe. Describe a recent situation where your actions revealed your faith in God. Why did you respond properly to that situation? Describe another recent situation where your actions revealed your lack of

faith in God. Why did you respond improperly to that situation? What did you learn from both situations that will help you the next time you face similar circumstances?

_____

_____

_____

Act

Create your own Bible confession sheet with verses that directly address a current need in your life. Spend fifteen minutes a day for a week meditating on and confessing these verses.

Memorize

It is written: "I believed; therefore I have spoken." With that same spirit of faith we also believe and therefore speak . . .

2 CORINTHIANS 4:13

CHAPTER 9

Faith in Action

Throughout this book, we have examined why you need faith, what it is, and how it grows. Now, let's look at some examples of faith in action.

Paul's Shipwreck

Sometime during the Apostle Paul's third missionary journey,[1] he decided to raise a contribution for the saints in Jerusalem. A serious rift had formed among the Jewish believers against Paul because he was offering the gospel to the Gentiles without circumcision. He was passionate about healing this divide, and so he determined to visit Jerusalem with both an offering from the Gentile churches and a team of representatives from among his Gentile converts. (Possibly, he thought it would be hard for the Jewish believers to remain mad at him after he had presented them with a big check.) He explained his purpose in the letter that he wrote to the Romans at this time.

> Now, however, I am on my way to Jerusalem in the service of the Lord's people there. For Macedonia and Achaia were pleased to make a contribution

---

[1] Luke records three distinct missionary journeys of Paul. The first was with Barnabas (Acts 13, 14). The second was with Silas (Acts 15:36-18:22). And the third was with several companions (Acts 18:23-21:17).

for the poor among the Lord's people in Jerusalem. They were pleased to do it, and indeed they owe it to them. For if the Gentiles have shared in the Jews' spiritual blessings, they owe it to the Jews to share with them their material blessings.

Romans 15:25-27

When Paul arrived in Jerusalem, angry Jews from Asia Minor incited the whole city against him and tried to kill him. The Roman military intervened, and after a series of trials, took him to prison in Caesarea. Two years later, after Paul had appealed to Caesar,[2] Festus, the Roman governor, placed him on a ship heading to Rome. But before the ship got very far, they encountered significant sailing difficulties.

Much time had been lost, and sailing had already become dangerous because by now it was after the Fast. So Paul warned them, "Men, I can see that our voyage is going to be disastrous and bring great loss to ship and cargo, and to our own lives also."

Acts 27:9,10

This was not necessarily a word of knowledge or prophecy on Paul's part. It was mostly common sense. Luke tells us that the Fast was already over, a reference to the Day of Atonement. The Day of Atonement was the last day of the Jewish feast of Tabernacles, and in 59 AD (the probable year of Paul's journey) the Day of Atonement came on October 5. In the first century, the dangerous season for sailing the Mediterranean began on

---

[2] One of the privileges of Roman citizenship was the right to appeal directly to Caesar if you were dissatisfied with the way you were being treated in a courtroom. Paul was born a Roman citizen and had this right.

September 14 and lasted until November 11. After that, all navigation on the open sea ceased for the winter.[3] It was now approaching the middle of October and Paul wisely urged them to winter where they were. They could then resume the journey in the spring, but the pilot and owner had different plans.

> But the centurion, instead of listening to what Paul said, followed the advice of the pilot and of the owner of the ship. Since the harbor was unsuitable to winter in, the majority decided that we should sail on, hoping to reach Phoenix and winter there.
>
> ACTS 27:11,12

As they set out, a gentle south wind was blowing and it appeared they would gain their purpose. But before very long, a wind of hurricane force swept down upon them. The ship was caught by the storm, and they gave way to it and were driven along. The ship took such a violent battering from the storm that the crew started throwing cargo out to stay afloat. After nearly two desperate weeks had passed, the sailors abandoned all hope of survival.

> When neither sun nor stars appeared for many days and the storm continued raging, we finally gave up all hope of being saved.
>
> ACTS 27:20

This was a very real storm that Paul and the others were in; it was not just a metaphor. But storms are often used throughout Scripture as metaphors for adversity and difficulties and the challenges of life.

---

[3] *F.F. Bruce*, Paul: Apostle of the Heart Set Free, *370.*

Here are a few examples:

. . . "Oh, that I had the wings of a dove! I would fly away and be at rest. . . . I would hurry to my place of shelter, far from the tempest and *storm*."

PSALM 55:6,8

You have been a refuge for the poor, a refuge for the needy in his distress, a shelter from the *storm* and a shade from the heat. . . .

ISAIAH 25:4

Paul was in this storm for two reasons. The first reason was because the centurion and company had disobeyed the wisdom of God. Paul, God's messenger, had warned them not to continue sailing, but they refused to listen. As a result, they were all in the storm. In the same way, there are times in our lives when the storm we are experiencing is the result of disobedience. Sometimes it is the disobedience of another (as in Paul's case), and sometimes it is our own disobedience. When we find ourselves in these situations, we need to discover where we missed God's will, repent, and start doing what He originally told us to do.

But there was a second reason Paul was in the storm: he was fulfilling his destiny. Paul was on his way to Rome to testify about the Lord Jesus Christ to Caesar, the most powerful man on earth. God had said to Ananias concerning Paul that he was ". . . *my chosen instrument to proclaim my name to the Gentiles and their kings*" (Acts 9:15). As the apostle to the Gentiles, he felt compelled to preach to Nero,[4] the leader of the Gentile world. And the devil would do anything he could to stop this meeting—even stirring up a huge storm.

---

[4] *Nero was the Caesar from 54 to 68 AD.*

Just like Paul's experience with this storm, there are also times in our lives when the storm we are experiencing is a result of fulfilling God's purpose. The enemy of our souls will stir up whatever he can to stop us from advancing toward fulfilling God's plan.

Many years ago, I found myself in a situation like this. I was experiencing a lot of pressure, and I did not know why. I did not know then what I know now about storms, and I could not figure out what the problem was. Exasperated, I set aside a time to seek God and to find out what was going on and what I needed to do about it. In desperation I cried, "God, what is my problem?"

The room became very still, and I had the sense that God was about to speak. And then, very softly in my heart, I heard these words, "Your problem is that you are right in the center of My will." That was a revelation to me. I assumed I had done something wrong. I assumed that if I was in God's will, everything would be peaceful. But after researching the Scriptures, I discovered that my assumptions were wrong. I discovered that sometimes the middle of God's will can feel like a terrible storm. Here are a few confirming verses:

> In fact, everyone who wants to live a godly life in Christ Jesus will be persecuted . . .
>
> 2 TIMOTHY 3:12

> . . . so that no one would be unsettled by these trials. For you know quite well that we are destined for them.
>
> 1 THESSALONIANS 3:3

> Join with me in suffering, like a good soldier of Christ Jesus.
>
> 2 TIMOTHY 2:3

What should we do when we find ourselves in a storm like that? We should follow Paul's example. The first thing he did was to find someone with a bigger problem than his.

> After they had gone a long time without food, Paul stood up before them and said: "Men, you should have taken my advice not to sail from Crete; then you would have spared yourselves this damage and loss. But now I urge you to keep up your courage, because not one of you will be lost; only the ship will be destroyed. Last night an angel of the God to whom I belong and whom I serve stood beside me and said, 'Do not be afraid, Paul. You must stand trial before Caesar; and God has graciously given you the lives of all who sail with you.'"
>
> ACTS 27:21-24

Whenever angels show up in response to someone's prayer, you can always tell what that person was praying about by what the angel says. In this example, the angel assured Paul that he would preach to Nero and that everyone on board would be saved. If that was the angel's answer, then Paul must have been praying for Nero and the men on board who did not know Christ. In the midst of a frightening and life-threatening storm, Paul refused to yield to fear or think about his own life. Instead, he found others needier than himself and prayed for them.

I have friends who pastored for many years in the southwest part of England. When I first visited them in 1995, their oldest son had recently been killed in a tragic accident while on the mission field. They were obviously under a deep burden of sorrow and despair. When I saw them again ten months later, it was also obvious that something had changed. Their countenance was bright and their outlook was positive. When we got a chance to talk, they told me what had happened.

They had realized that if they did not do something about the way they were feeling, it was going to destroy them. So they purchased a subscription to the local paper and started scanning the obituary column everyday looking for parents who had lost a child. When they found someone, they would put together a care package and show up on their doorstep. When the grieving parents came to the door, they would introduce themselves and say, "We also lost a child not long ago and we know what you are going through. If you want someone to talk with or pray with or just cry with, we are here."

Not surprisingly, they had the opportunity to pray for several people and lead them to faith in Christ. In the worst storm of their lives, they found others with bigger problems than theirs. As a result, they were able to triumph over their own storm.

The next thing Paul did was he found God's purpose in the storm. He said to the entire crew:

". . . we *must* run aground on some island."

ACTS 27:26

Notice his word choice: *"must."* There was an island that Paul had to go to. Why? Because there was something he had to do there.

Paul, in all likelihood, would never have visited Malta if not for this storm. It was not a prominent place in the Roman empire, and it was not somewhere you normally went. But because of this storm, Paul ended up there. As a result of his visit, the gospel was preached and a church established on the island. There has been a continuous Christian witness on that island ever since.

Sometimes storms in our lives take us to places we never intended to go and never would have gone on our own. But God works in His sovereign way to accomplish His purpose in our lives, even through events that, at the time, we may think are working against us.

The final thing Paul did in the storm was to say what God said about it.

"So keep up your courage, men, for I have faith in God that it will happen just as he told me."

ACTS 27:25

There was a man of faith on that ship, and he had a Word from God. Although Paul was the prisoner, he stood boldly on the deck of the ship and spoke God's Word with confidence. In any storm of life, we should follow Paul's example. Find out what God has to say about our storm, and then boldly proclaim His Word without wavering. It will turn out for us just as He said!

Joshua and Caleb

Then Caleb silenced the people before Moses and said, "We should go up and take possession of the land, for we can certainly do it." But the men who had gone up with him said, "We can't attack those people; they are stronger than we are." And they spread among the Israelites a bad report about the land they had explored. They said, "The land we explored devours those living in it. All the people we saw there are of great size. We saw the Nephilim there (the descendants of Anak come from the Nephilim). We seemed like grasshoppers in our own eyes, and we looked the same to them." That night all the members of the community raised their voices and wept aloud. All the Israelites grumbled against Moses and Aaron, and the whole assembly said to them, "If only we had died in Egypt! Or in this wilderness! Why is the LORD bringing us to this land only to let us fall by the sword? Our wives and children will be taken as plunder. Wouldn't it be better for us to go back to Egypt?" And they said to each other, "We should choose a leader and go back to Egypt."

Numbers 13:30-14:4

This historical event takes place sometime around 1450 BC. Moses had recently delivered God's people from Egyptian slavery and was attempting to take them into the promised land. God had given the people a promise, and they had a covenant with Him—the land was theirs. But there was a problem: there were giants in the land.

There are always giants in the land. There are always obstacles standing in the way of the promises of God. Someone once said, "Obstacles are those frightful things you see when you take your eyes off your goals." That quote would be more accurate if it was rewritten to say, "Obstacles are those frightful things you see when you take your eyes off God's Word." If living by faith was easy, everyone would do it. The Apostle Paul understood this, and he knew that the example of the Israelites was a warning to us all.

> For I do not want you to be ignorant of the fact, brothers and sisters, that our ancestors were all under the cloud and that they all passed through the sea. They were all baptized into Moses in the cloud and in the sea. They all ate the same spiritual food and drank the same spiritual drink; for they drank from the spiritual rock that accompanied them, and that rock was Christ. Nevertheless, God was not pleased with most of them; their bodies were scattered in the wilderness.
>
> 1 Corinthians 10:1-5

The primary warning to us in this passage is: "God was not pleased with *most* of them." Why was He not pleased? Because they did not believe His promise, and without faith it is impossible to please Him. What was the result of their unbelief? *Their bodies were scattered in the wilderness.* Unbelief has serious consequences. Paul knew that, and he wanted to warn us. He said:

> Do you not know that in a race all the runners run,
> but only one gets the prize? Run in such a way as to
> get the prize.
>
> 1 CORINTHIANS 9:24

I still remember the first time I read this verse. I was a new believer with little prior Bible knowledge. I also tended to be excessively literal in my interpretation of Scripture. So I was shocked when I read the words, *only one gets the prize.* How could that be? Only one person? I thought, "Is that one per city, or one per church, or just one?" I wasn't sure exactly what the prize was or how many people could qualify for it, but I determined at that moment that if only one was going to get it, that one would be me.

Years later, I realized that although my hermeneutical methodology[5] was all wrong, I had actually come close to understanding Paul's intended meaning. He was not saying that only one wins the prize. He was saying that we ought to run *as if* only one wins the prize. And it would make a difference, wouldn't it, in the way we pursued the things of God if there was only one winner? Obstacles would not have the same power over our lives.

A high school football coach told a story that illustrates this idea. His team was competing for the State Championship against their rivals. They were leading 6-0 with time left for only one play. He instructed his quarterback to take the snap and down the ball. Time would run out, and they would be the champions.

But his quarterback had ambitions, and he felt like his many talents had not been fully displayed in such a low scoring game.

---

[5] *Hermeneutics is the science of accurate biblical interpretation.*

So the quarterback changed the play and called for a pass play instead. After receiving the snap, he located his receiver in the open and threw a perfect spiral to him. But at the last minute the defensive player stepped in front of the pass, intercepted it, and took off for the end zone. It looked like he would score a touchdown when at the last possible minute he was tackled from behind—by the quarterback.

Later, the two coaches discussed the last play. The losing coach was incredulous that a slow-footed quarterback could catch his fleet-footed defensive back, especially when his player had a head start. The winning coach explained it to him in simple terms: "Your player was running for a touchdown and a State Championship, but my player was running for *his life!*"

How you run does make a difference.

How do we run in such a way as to get the prize? We follow the example of Joshua and Caleb. Out of that whole generation of Israelites, they were the only two people who received God's promise. The people of Israel did not win the prize and enter the land because they believed in the giants more than they believed in the promise, and only people of faith inherit the land. God's testimony concerning the faith of Caleb was:

> "But because my servant Caleb has a different spirit and follows me wholeheartedly, I will bring him into the land he went to, and his descendants will inherit it."
>
> NUMBERS 14:24

Joshua and Caleb gave us an example to follow.

- They believed God's promises more than they believed the testimony of their physical senses.

- They declared God's promises while facing great obstacles.

We all have our own personal giants that continually try to deter us from our promised land. But if we follow the faith of Joshua and Caleb, we will win the prize.

Jairus and the Woman

A large crowd gathered around Jesus expecting Him to do miracles. People had come from miles around, bringing their sick with them. They were all watching and waiting and hoping. But through the middle of the crowd came a man who could not wait. His daughter was dying and he was determined to have Jesus heal her.

> Then one of the synagogue leaders, named Jairus, came, and when he saw Jesus, he fell at his feet. He pleaded earnestly with him, "My little daughter is dying. Please come and put your hands on her so that she will be healed and live."
>
> MARK 5:22,23

"... she *will be* healed," he said. Jairus was certain. His faith was unwavering.

If Jesus was politically correct, He would have instructed Jairus to wait his turn. There were many who had been there longer than he. Jairus would have to wait—it was only fair. But that is not what happened.

> So Jesus went with him. A large crowd followed and pressed around him.
>
> MARK 5:24

Jesus responds to faith. There were many that day that had needs, some probably as great as that of Jairus, but none of them received help. Jairus received a miracle, but everyone else went home disappointed. Well, not quite everyone. There was one other person who believed that day. She also received a miracle.

Life had been difficult for this woman. She had been subject to bleeding for twelve years. Many doctors had promised a cure, but they had just taken her money and treated her badly. She was worse now than when she started.

But then she heard about Jesus. They said He could heal the sick, cure the lame, and raise the dead. And as she listened to the stories, something began to happen within her. Faith was born and began to grow. Finally, she determined she would go to Jesus and receive her healing.

When she approached Jesus that day, she kept saying to herself what she had probably said so many times before, "If I just touch His garments, I will be healed. If I just touch His garments, I *will* be healed." As Jesus passed by, she reached out and touched His garment.

Immediately her bleeding stopped and she felt in her body that she was freed from her suffering.

Mark 5:29

Hundreds had pressed against Jesus that day, and hundreds had touched His garments. But there was something different about this woman. She really believed.

At once Jesus realized that power had gone out from him. He turned around in the crowd and asked, "Who touched my clothes?" "You see the people crowding against you," his disciples answered, "and yet you can ask, 'Who touched me?'" But Jesus kept looking around to see who had done it. Then the woman, knowing what had happened to her, came and fell at his feet and, trembling with fear, told him the whole truth. He said to her, "Daughter, your faith has healed you. Go in peace and be freed from your suffering."

MARK 5:30-34

She put her faith in action and received a miracle from Jesus that day.

While Jesus was delayed with the woman, men came from the home of Jairus with the news he had dreaded, *"Your daughter is dead . . . why bother the teacher anymore?"*

Ignoring the bad report, Jesus said to Jairus, *"Don't be afraid; just believe."*

Jairus obviously did what Jesus told him to do because before the day was over, Jairus was eating a meal with his twelve-year-old daughter.

Jairus put his faith in action and received a miracle from Jesus that day.

Conclusion

Faith requires action. Men and women in the Bible put their faith in action as a testimony for us to follow their example.

APPLICATION

Discuss

1. Have you ever experienced a storm in your life as the result of disobedience? What did you do to get out of it? Have you ever experienced a storm in your life as the result of following God's destiny for your life? What did you learn from it that will help you the next time a storm comes?

_____

_____

_____

2. In the midst of a great storm, Paul boldly declared God's Word concerning the situation. Do you find it difficult to speak God's Word when you are in the middle of a storm? Why? What can you do to correct this and change?

_____

_____

_____

3. What would change about your life if Paul's statement in 1 Corinthians 9:24 was literal and only one got the prize? What should change in your life now that you know he is saying that we ought to run as if only one wins the prize? What action steps will you take immediately to institute those changes?

_____

_____

_____

4. What are the main giants in your life right now that are keeping you from inheriting your promised land? What will you do to defeat them?

_____

_____

_____

Act
Read Acts 27. Find as many principles of faith in the text as you can. Select one and create a plan to implement it in your life.

Memorize
"So keep up your courage, men, for I have faith in God that it will happen just as he told me."

ACTS 27:25

APPENDIX A

The Bible

General Facts

- The word "Bible" comes from the Greek word *biblos* which simply means "book." The Bible is "the Book."
- Over forty different authors from diverse vocations on three continents wrote the Bible over a period of more than 1500 years. They used a variety of literary types, including history, law (civil, criminal, ethical, ritual), poetry, treatise, philosophical musing, parable, wisdom literature, narrative, diatribe, allegory, biography, personal correspondence, travelogue, prophecy, and apocalyptic literature.
- The Bible has been translated into more languages than any book in the world. According to the Statistical Summary provided by the United Bible Societies' World Report, as of March 2002, the whole Bible had been translated into 392 languages and dialects, and parts of it into another 1,895.[1]
- In the thirteenth century, Stephen Langton, the archbishop of Canterbury, divided the Bible into the chapter divisions we use today. In 1551, Robert Estienne (sometimes referred to as Robert Stephens or just

---

[1] Biblica, *http://www.ibsstl.org/bibles/about/19.php.*

Stephanus) added the verse references found in all modern Bibles.

- The Old Testament was written primarily in Hebrew (a few sections were written in Aramaic[2]). The New Testament was written in common marketplace Greek (not classical or modern Greek).

- There are sixty-six books in the Bible: thirty-nine in the Old Testament, and twenty-seven in the New Testament.

- The first five books of the Old Testament are called the Pentateuch.[3]

- The Old Testament is divided into three parts: history, poetry, and prophecy. There are seventeen history books,[4] five poetry books,[5] and seventeen prophecy books.[6]

- The New Testament is divided into four parts: gospel,[7] history, epistle, and apocalypse.

- The Gospels are accounts of the life and ministry of Jesus Christ, arranged not as a biography or chronological narrative,[8] but as a theological sermon to meet the needs of a particular group.

---

[2] *The Aramaic portions of the Old Testament are the following: Ezra 4:8 through 6:18; 7:11-26; Daniel 2:4 through 7:28; Genesis 31:47 (two words); Jeremiah 10:11. The language in which they are written used to be called Chaldee, but is now generally known simply as Biblical Aramaic* (International Standard Bible Encyclopedia).

[3] *The word Pentateuch comes from two Greek words: penta, which means "five," and teuch, which means "book." The term was first used by Origen to denote what the Jews of his time called the Torah (teaching). The Torah is the holiest and most beloved of the sacred writings of the Jews* (Microsoft® Encarta® Reference Library 2002).

[4] *Genesis, Exodus, Leviticus, Numbers, Deuteronomy, Joshua, Judges, Ruth, 1 & 2 Samuel, 1 & 2 Kings, 1 & 2 Chronicles, Ezra, Nehemiah, and Esther.*

[5] *Job, Psalms, Proverbs, Ecclesiastes, and Song of Songs.*

[6] *The five major prophetic books are: Isaiah, Jeremiah, Lamentations, Ezekiel, Daniel. The twelve minor prophets are: Hosea, Joel, Amos, Obadiah, Jonah, Micah, Nahum, Habakkuk, Zephaniah, Haggai, Zechariah, and Malachi.*

[7] *The Gospels are often included under the history heading.*

[8] *A Gospel includes biography and chronological narrative, but that is not its primary purpose.*

- The Gospels record material that is historical, but cannot be considered historical in the same way the term is used today. Apart from Luke, the Gospels do not claim to be chronological. They contain very little information about Christ's early life and spend an excessive amount of time reporting the events of the Passion Week.

- The first three Gospels (Matthew, Mark, and Luke) are similar to one another in structure, content, and wording. They are called the Synoptics (from a Greek word meaning "to see together"). They concentrate on Jesus' Galilean ministry and public discourses. The fourth Gospel, John, concentrates on His Judean ministry and private discourses.

- There is one book of history: Acts. Luke's history had a limited scope. He did not focus on the biographies of the apostles, church organization, or the general growth of the Church. Instead, he showed how the Church expanded from the isolated city of Jerusalem to the great metropolis of Rome.

- There are twenty-one Epistles.[9] The epistle was a common literary form in the first century Greco-Roman world. It usually consisted of a standard greeting, thanksgiving, message, and farewell.

- There is one Apocalypse: Revelation. Apocalypse, a genre popular in the first century, concerns the end of the world and the salvation of the righteous. It uses an abundance of symbols, visions, and prophecies.

---

[9] *Thirteen books are called Pauline: Romans, 1 & 2 Corinthians, Galatians, Ephesians, Philippians, Colossians, 1 & 2 Thessalonians, 1 & 2 Timothy, Titus, Philemon; and eight are called general: Hebrews, James, 1 & 2 Peter, 1, 2, & 3 John, and Jude.*

The Formulation of the Canon

The word "canon" comes from a Greek word meaning a "measuring rod." It is used to describe the inspired books of the Bible. The word "canonicity" refers to the process whereby the early Church Fathers determined which books were divinely inspired and had the seal of divine authority. The New Testament Canon was the result of 350 years of prayer and research.[10] Many forces contributed to its final form. Here are a few of them:

- There was a need for an authoritative voice to proclaim the message of the apostles who were all dead by the end of the first century. Oral tradition would continue to deteriorate over the years, and they needed a written canon for accurate instruction because there were many spurious writings claiming to be inspired. For example, the Apocalypse of Adam, the Gospel of Philip,[11] the Acts of Peter, the Acts of Thomas, etc.
- There was a need to know which books were authoritative for doctrine, and which were merely edifying. For example, what should be done with Clement's letter to the Corinthians, written in 95 AD? A number of the churches reasoned that since Clement was a disciple of Paul (Philippians 4:3), the letter should be authorita-

---

[10] *The final form of the canon developed gradually. Clement of Rome (95) mentioned at least eight New Testament books in a letter. Polycarp (108) acknowledged fifteen letters. Irenaeus (185) acknowledged twenty-one books. Hippolytus (170-235) recognized twenty-two books. The Muratorian Canon (170) included all the New Testament books except Hebrews, James, and 3 John. Athanasius (367) cited the twenty-seven books of the New Testament as being the only true books. The Council of Laodicea (363), the Council of Hippo (393) and the Council of Carthage (397) all affirmed that only the twenty-seven books of the New Testament were to be read in the churches. "When the Synod of Hippo listed the twenty-seven books of the New Testament, it did not confer upon them any authority which they did not already possess, but simply recorded their previously established canonicity." (F.F. Bruce, The Books and the Parchments, 113.)*

[11] *Referred to frequently in the runaway bestseller The DaVinci Code as the "sacred text" that explains the truth about the marriage of Jesus and Mary Magdalene.*

tive. (In the end, Clement's letter was rightly considered merely edifying and not canonical.)

- There was a need for a true canon to answer the false ones developing. For example, the canon that the heretic Marcion[12] established around 150 AD.
- There was a need to establish finality in revelation. Various sects and cults propagated ideas of continuing revelation and new messages coming from God.
- There was a need to decide which books to die for. For example, in 302, the emperor Diocletian issued an edict to uproot Christianity by burning Bibles and destroying churches. Christians caught with the sacred books could be killed.

There were at least four tests applied to the various books to determine their authenticity.

- The first was apostolicity: Was the author an apostle or did he have a connection with an apostle? Mark was not considered an apostle, but he wrote under Peter's authority. Luke also was not considered an apostle, but he wrote under Paul's authority.
- The second was acceptance: Did the church at large accept the book? By this rule, spurious or false books were rejected. However, this rule also delayed the recognition of some legitimate books. For example, James, Jude, 2 Peter, and Revelation were some of the last books accepted into the canon because not all the churches initially recognized their inspiration.

---

[12] Marcion rejected the Old Testament and removed all New Testament writings apart from Paul's letters and parts of Luke's Gospel.

- The third was content: Was the book consistent with orthodox teaching?
- The fourth was inspiration: Did the book reflect the quality of inspiration?

Understanding the Bible

- There are five concepts we must be familiar with to have a proper understanding of the Bible: revelation, inspiration, inerrancy, illumination, and interpretation.
- Revelation means that God manifests Himself to particular persons at definite times and places, enabling those persons to enter into a redemptive relationship with Him.[13] There are two kinds of revelation: general and special.
- General revelation is God's communication of Himself to all persons at all times and in all places.[14] Special revelation is God's authoritative Word conveyed objectively and propositionally through the exclusive medium of the Bible.[15]
- John Calvin explained the difference between the two with this analogy: "Just as old men with weak vision, if you thrust before them a most beautiful volume, even if they recognize it to be some sort of writing, yet can

---

[13] *"Nobody would know the truth about God, or be able to relate to Him in a personal way, had not God first acted to make Himself known." (J.I. Packer, Concise Theology: A Guide to Historic Christian Beliefs.)*

[14] *There are three manifestations of general revelation. <u>Nature</u> reveals God's glory (Romans 1:20). <u>Providence</u> reveals God's love (Matthew 5:45). <u>Conscience</u> reveals God's holiness (Romans 2:14-15).*

[15] *There are three other manifestations of special revelation. The first is miraculous events—God manifesting Himself in history. (For example, the parting of the Red Sea.) The second is divine speech—God revealing Himself through human language. (For example, Joseph's dream to move his family to Egypt until the death of Herod.) The third is visible manifestations—God showing Himself in visible form. (For example, the Lord appearing to Abraham by the oaks of Mamre in Genesis 18.)*

scarcely construe two words, but with the aid of spectacles will begin to read distinctly; so Scripture, gathering up the otherwise confused knowledge of God in our minds, having dispersed our dullness, clearly shows us the true God. This is a special gift of God to instruct the church."[16]

- Inspiration is the supernatural influence on the Bible authors, making their writings infallible and an exact expression of God's mind and will[17] (2 Peter 1:20,21; 2 Timothy 3:16,17). The authors retained their individual personalities as thinkers and writers.

- Inerrancy means that the Bible is fully true in all it teaches and affirms.[18] Inerrancy allows for popular expressions, approximations, phenomenal language, and variety in details in explaining the same event. It also allows for variety in style. John's Gospel was written in the simple style of an unlearned fisherman; Luke's Gospel was written with the sophisticated vocabulary of an educated person; Paul's Epistles were written with the logic of a debater.

- Illumination is the ministry of the Holy Spirit whereby He enlightens those who are in a right relationship with Him to comprehend the written Word of God. The Bible is God-breathed and is qualitatively different from all other literature. Therefore, it is necessary that man receive God-given help in understanding the Bible (1 Corinthians 2:11,14; Luke 24:45).

---

[16] *John Calvin,* Institutes of the Christian Religion *I, 6.1.*

[17] *"Inspiration is the supernatural influence exerted on the sacred writers by the Spirit of God, by virtue of which their writings are given Divine trustworthiness."* (International Standard Bible Encyclopedia, *Volume 3, 1453.)*

[18] *The Scriptures possess the quality of freedom from error. They are exempt from the liability to mistake, incapable of error. In all their teachings they are in perfect accord with the truth"* (E.J. Young, Thy Word is Truth, *113.)*

- Interpretation is the human process of cooperating with the divine process of illumination. It is the careful and systematic analysis of a text to discover the intended meaning. The goal of interpretation is to determine the meaning of the text in its original context—what the author meant when he wrote to his original readers.

Interpretation

"The Bible's central message is so plainly stated that the most unlearned of those who have ears to hear and eyes to see can understand it. The technicalities of scholarship may be out of the ordinary Bible reader's reach, but none the less he can, with God's blessing, grasp all the main truths of God's message."[19]

There are several requirements for a proper understanding of Scripture.

The first requirement to accurately interpret Scripture is a careful reading of the literary context of the passage. The literary context is what precedes a passage and what follows it. The immediate context of a passage is the paragraph and chapter in which it occurs. The remote context of a passage is the book and testament in which it occurs.

The second requirement to accurately interpret Scripture is an understanding of the historical context of the passage. The Bible was written by God; therefore it has eternal relevance. The Bible was also written by men; therefore it has historical specificity. Therefore, knowledge of the specific time and place

---

[19]   J. I. Packer, Fundamentalism and the Word of God, 107.

in which the authors lived and the specific context they wrote in will provide a deeper understanding of a passage.

A major obstacle to understanding the Bible is that we are separated from the historical events by thousands of years. The Bible is a record of the words God spoke through real people in real circumstances in real places at real times. Therefore, every verse has an historical context that determines the meaning of the verse. The more accurately we reconstruct the historical setting, the more accurately we will understand God's Word. The more we understand what God's Word meant to the original hearers, the more we will understand what it means to us.

There are five significant factors in considering the historical context of a passage.

- Who wrote the original document? For example, John Mark was the author of the second Gospel. The Church Father Papias said, "Mark, who became Peter's interpreter, wrote accurately, though not in order, all that he remembered of the things said or done by the Lord. For he had neither heard the Lord nor been one of His followers, but afterwards, he had followed Peter . . ." So Mark's Gospel is a presentation of Peter's view of Jesus.
- Why was the original document written? For example, 1 Corinthians was written in response to questions from the church (7:1,25; 8:1; 12:1; 16:1), and reports that Paul had received about problems in the church (1:11).
- When was the original document written? For example, 2 Timothy was written shortly before Paul was beheaded on the Ostian Way outside of Rome. The book contains a record of the things that were uppermost on

the mind of the great apostle before his departure from this world.

- Who was the original document written to? For example, the Philippians became Paul's most faithful financial partners. They sent contributions when he was in Thessalonica (Philippians 4:16), a contribution when he was in Corinth (2 Corinthians 11:9), a contribution to his offering for the saints in Jerusalem (2 Corinthians 8:1-5), and an offering during his Roman imprisonment (Philippians 4:18). No wonder Paul could say with such confidence to them, *And my God shall supply all your needs according to His riches in glory in Christ Jesus.*

- What were the culture, politics, and geography of the city or region that received the original document?

  Culture: Corinth was one of the most sinful cities in the Roman Empire. Its main tourist attraction was the Temple to Aphrodite with its 1,000 cult prostitutes. The Greek playwright Aristophanes coined the verb "to corinthianize," a slang term for fornication, because of the sensuality of the city. So when Paul said, *It is actually reported that there is sexual immorality among you, and of a kind that does not occur even among pagans . . .* it was a stinging rebuke to a city already known for its sexual excess.

  Politics: When the Jewish elders caught a woman in adultery they thought they had discovered the perfect way to trap Jesus. They said, *"Teacher, this woman was caught in the act of adultery. In the Law Moses commanded us to stone such women. Now what do you say?"* They were using this question as a trap, in order to have a basis for accusing Him. The Romans allowed a measure of self-government in the territories they controlled, but they withheld the right of capital punishment. If Jesus upheld the Law of Moses, He would be in opposition to Rome and guilty of treason. If He denied the Law of Moses, He would lose favor with the people. His answer sidestepped both pitfalls and enabled Him to extend grace and forgiveness to the adulterous woman.

Geography: Laodicea was one of the most prosperous cities in all of Asia Minor. But it had one major drawback: no local water supply. Its two neighbors, Colossae and Hieropolis, had cold well water and hot springs. But Laodicea was dependent upon water delivered through a system of stone pipes from a spring six miles away. By the time the water arrived it was neither hot (like Hieropolis) nor cold (like Colossae) but lukewarm—mineral-laden and well-suited to induce vomiting. That helps explain Jesus' words in Revelation 3:15,16 (NASB): *"I know your deeds, that you are neither cold nor hot; I wish that you were cold or hot. So because you are lukewarm, and neither hot nor cold, I will spit* (Lit. vomit) *you out of My mouth."*

The third requirement to accurately interpret Scripture is an understanding of the different literary styles. To correctly understand a given text's original meaning, knowing its literary form is helpful. You do not read poetry the same way you would read a legal document. Each literary genre has its own unique characteristics.

The fourth requirement to accurately interpret Scripture is an awareness of our prejudices. We come to the text with many of our own ideas. The culture we were raised in shapes our perceptions of many of the issues addressed in the Bible. The religious institutions in which we have participated also shape our views on many topics of the Bible.

Reading the Bible

The first and primary way we ingest the Word is through reading. Reading the Bible gives us a general overview of God's Word. It also gives God a medium to speak to us, either during the reading, or later when the Holy Spirit quickens appropriate verses.

The Bible can be read using the fast method or the slow method. Each method has a different purpose and objective. The purpose of the fast method is to gain an overall understanding of the historical development and message of the Bible. The objective is knowledge. The purpose of the slow method is to reflect deeply on smaller sections of the Bible. The objective is understanding.

John Wesley taught several tips for effective Bible reading:[20]

- Set apart time every morning and evening for the purpose of reading.
- Read with a determination to know the whole will of God and with a steady resolution to do it.
- Pray seriously and earnestly before consulting the Word of God, because Scripture can only be under-

---

[20] John Wesley, Preface to Explanatory Notes upon the Old Testament.

stood through the same Spirit whereby it was given. Scripture reading should also end with prayer so that what was read might be written on the heart.

- Pause frequently and examine your heart and life by what you read.
- Whatever light you receive should be used to the uttermost and immediately. Let there be no delay. Whatever you resolve, begin to execute the first moment you can.

Reading the Bible naturally leads to memorization. Jesus obviously memorized Scripture because He was able to defeat the devil in the wilderness (with no scrolls readily available) by quoting the Bible. The following are some tips for memorization:[21]

- Memorize verses that relate to what God is currently saying to you.
- Read the verse aloud and write it out, many times if necessary.
- Write out the verse with the reference on a "flash card."
- Always memorize verses word perfect.
- Emphasize key words in the verse when quoting.

---

[21] *Modified from* Scripture Memory: Your Key to Success, *Monica Best, http://www.fsbcdc.org.*

APPENDIX B

Questions about Suffering

T here is a good bit of confusion concerning suffering and the life of faith. In this section, we will attempt to answer some of the more prominent questions about this topic.

Does a life of faith automatically guarantee the absence of suffering?

It depends how you define suffering. Suffering is a comprehensive term and, unfortunately, we have a tendency to lump every kind of suffering into one category. There are some types of suffering that a person living the life of faith should not experience. And there are some types of suffering that a person living the life of faith will experience—even to a greater degree than if he or she was not living by faith.

Are there extreme views concerning suffering?

There are two extreme views regarding suffering and both of them should be avoided. The first view is that all suffering is good and should be embraced. Therefore, all suffering is redemptive. In this view, God is the author of the suffering and any attempt to resist the suffering is actually resisting the will of God.

The second view is that all suffering is bad and should be resisted. In this view, the devil and evil men are the authors of all suffering and any passivity toward suffering is disobedience to the will of God.

Both of these extreme views have surfaced throughout the long centuries of Church history, but the first view has been the most prominent.

What different kinds of suffering are recorded in the Bible?

- There is suffering that is the result of personal disobedience to God's Word and His Will.

  > Some sat in darkness, in utter darkness, prisoners suffering in iron chains, because they rebelled against God's commands and despised the plans of the Most High.
  >
  > PSALM 107:10,11

- There is suffering that is the result of someone else's disobedience.

  > Your children will be shepherds here for forty years, suffering for your unfaithfulness, until the last of your bodies lies in the wilderness.
  >
  > NUMBERS 14:33

- There is suffering that is demonically inspired.

  > Resist him, standing firm in the faith, because you know that the family of believers through-

out the world is undergoing the same kind of sufferings.

1 PETER 5:9

- There is suffering that is inflicted upon us by other people.

> She had suffered a great deal under the care of many doctors and had spent all she had, yet instead of getting better she grew worse.
>
> MARK 5:26

Each of the above categories of suffering should be resisted with God's Word and His promises.

Is there a kind of suffering that is according to the will of God?

Yes. The following is a partial list of Scriptures.

> So then, those who suffer according to God's will should commit themselves to their faithful Creator and continue to do good.
>
> 1 PETER 4:19

> Not only so, but we also glory in our sufferings, because we know that suffering produces perseverance . . .
>
> ROMANS 5:3

So do not be ashamed of the testimony about our Lord or of me his prisoner. Rather, join with me in suffering for the gospel, by the power of God.

2 TIMOTHY 1:8

However, if you suffer as a Christian, do not be ashamed, but praise God that you bear that name.

1 PETER 4:16

For it has been granted to you on behalf of Christ not only to believe in him, but also to suffer for him . . .

PHILIPPIANS 1:29

"I will show him how much he must suffer for my name."

ACTS 9:16

I want to know Christ—yes, to know the power of his resurrection and participation in his sufferings, becoming like him in his death . . .

PHILIPPIANS 3:10

As the above list shows us, there is an abundance of evidence that suffering has a significant place in the life of faith. We should expect this to be true when we look at the life of our Lord.

In bringing many sons and daughters to glory, it was fitting that God, for whom and through whom everything exists, should make the pioneer of their salvation perfect through what he suffered.

HEBREWS 2:10

He was despised and rejected by mankind, a man of suffering, and familiar with pain. Like one from whom people hide their faces he was despised, and we held him in low esteem.

ISAIAH 53:3

More evidence that suffering fits into a life of faith is seen in Hebrews 11, the great faith chapter. The context of the chapter was the suffering the Hebrew believers were experiencing. The author attempted to encourage them by recounting the example of men and women of faith who had experienced great challenges and suffering in their own lives.

Another example is evident in Paul's defense of his apostolic credentials to the Corinthians. When forced to prove his apostolic credentials, he provided a list of his many sufferings. What an interesting response! Most ministers today would defend their calling with a list of their achievements and accomplishments. But Paul listed his sufferings.

. . . I have worked much harder, been in prison more frequently, been flogged more severely, and been exposed to death again and again. Five times I received from the Jews the forty lashes minus one. Three times I was beaten with rods, once I was pelted with stones, three times I was shipwrecked, I spent a night and a day in the open sea, I have been constantly on the move. I have been in danger from rivers, in danger from bandits, in danger from my fellow Jews, in danger from Gentiles; in danger in the city, in danger in the country, in danger at sea; and in danger from false believers. I have labored and toiled and have often gone without sleep; I have known hunger and thirst and have often gone without food; I have been cold and naked. Besides everything else, I face daily the pressure of my concern for all the churches.

2 CORINTHIANS 11:23-28

George Muller said this about suffering and the life of faith:

"I say—and say it deliberately—trials, obstacles, difficulties, and sometimes defeats, are the very food of Faith. I get letters from so many of God's dear children who say: 'Dear Brother Muller, I'm writing this because I am so weak in faith.' Just so surely as we ask to have our Faith strengthened, we must feel a willingness to take from God's hand the means for strengthening it. We must allow Him to educate us through trials and bereavements and troubles. It is through trials that Faith is exercised and developed more and more. God affectionately permits difficulties, that He may develop unceasingly that which He is willing to do for us . . ."

What are some examples of suffering according to the will of God?

- When we are persecuted for our faith.

  The apostles left the Sanhedrin, rejoicing because they had been counted worthy of suffering disgrace for the Name.

  ACTS 5:41

In October 2000, a nineteen-year-old Christian student was arrested along with over twenty others in China. They were arrested for studying and teaching the Word of God. Each person was beaten and released. The nineteen-year-old was kept and beaten daily as an example to others who might be interested in following the same path. The young man was systematically beaten daily in front of others for twenty-eight days until he died. The police felt this would be a definite blow against Christianity in the region.

They were wrong. Over 10,000 letters came into the police station within days of the young man's death stating they, after seeing the courage and strength of the young man, now had greater faith than ever before and they were identifying themselves to the police as Christians.

- When we are called upon to take up our cross.

    In 2005, I wrote the following article on my website:

    I put my nineteen-year-old daughter on a plane to South Africa last month. She is serving in an AIDS orphanage for nine weeks. It was not too emotional for me because I knew she would be home soon. But I wonder how I would feel if she returned with news that God had called her to move to South Africa permanently? At present, it is just an exciting missions adventure; then it would be a major life change. Am I ready for that?

A few days after contemplating this possibility, I was researching the life of Francis Asbury, the first leader of the Methodist church in America. When Asbury was twenty-six, he responded to John Wesley's call for missionaries to go to America. As he boarded the ship for America, his devout Methodist father wept openly, fearing he would never see his son again.

He never did.

It cut me to the heart when I read that story. I wondered how painful it would be to say goodbye to your son for the last time.

Fortunately, travel has improved since 1771. If my daughter left, I would certainly see her again. But not nearly enough. And what about when she marries and has children? How often would I see my grandchildren?

While reflecting on these things I turned to Jesus' call to discipleship.

> "Anyone who loves their father or mother more than me is not worthy of me; anyone who loves their son or daughter more than me is not worthy of me. Whoever does not take up their cross and follow me is not worthy of me."
>
> MATTHEW 10:37,38

I first read these words thirty years ago when I responded to the call to make Jesus the Lord of my life. I was a nineteen-year-old college student with hardly a penny to my name. Sure, I had to surrender everything to Him, but there was not much to surrender. But it is different now.

Jesus still wants everything, but it seems there is a lot more to give.

Discipleship gets more costly every year.

On December 13, 2008, my daughter married a South African rugby player, Ernie Kruger. Two weeks later, she boarded a plane to leave for her new life in South Africa. I had no idea when she first left in 2005 that my article would prove to be prophetic.

Is there an answer for human suffering?

Yes. God understands our suffering and is concerned about it.

> The LORD said, "I have indeed seen the misery of my people in Egypt. I have heard them crying out because of their slave drivers, and I am concerned about their suffering."
>
> EXODUS 3:7

> For he has not despised or scorned the suffering of the afflicted one; he has not hidden his face from him but has listened to his cry for help.
>
> PSALM 22:24

Not only is He concerned, but He has an answer: His Word and His promises.

"But those who suffer he delivers in their suffering;
he speaks to them in their affliction."

JOB 36:15

My comfort in my suffering is this: Your promise pre-
serves my life.

PSALM 119:50

But the best answer to human suffering is the knowledge
that *our light and momentary troubles are achieving for us an
eternal glory that far outweighs them all* (2 Corinthians 4:17).

Now if we are children, then we are heirs—heirs
of God and co-heirs with Christ, if indeed we share
in his sufferings in order that we may also share in
his glory. I consider that our present sufferings are
not worth comparing with the glory that will be revealed in us.

ROMANS 8:17,18

APPENDIX C

Scriptural Confessions

Wisdom and Revelation[1]

The God of my Lord Jesus Christ, the Father of Glory, has given me a spirit of wisdom and revelation in the true knowledge of Him. The eyes of my heart have been flooded with light, so that I might know what is the hope of His calling, what are the riches of the glory of His inheritance in the saints, and what is the surpassing greatness of His power toward us who believe.

I am filled with the knowledge of His will in all spiritual wisdom and understanding. The Spirit of truth has come to guide me into all truth and to disclose, unveil, divulge, and reveal to me what is to come. He is teaching me all things and bringing all things to my remembrance.

I receive His sayings, I treasure His commands within me, I make my ear attentive to wisdom, I incline my heart to understanding; I cry for discernment, I lift my voice for understanding; I seek her as silver and search for her as hidden treasures. Then I will discern the fear of the Lord and discover the knowledge of God. For He gives wisdom; from His mouth come knowledge and understanding.

---

[1] *Adapted from Ephesians 1:17-19; Colossians 1:9; 2:3,10; John 14:26; 16:13; Proverbs 2:1-6; Daniel 2:22,23; 1 Corinthians 2:9-12; James 1:5; Mark 4:22; Luke 21:15.*

In Christ are hidden all the treasures of wisdom and knowledge; and in Him I have been made complete. It is He who reveals the profound and hidden things; He knows what is in the darkness, and the light dwells with Him. To Him I give thanks and praise, for He has given me wisdom and power.

Things which an eye has not seen and an ear has not heard and has not entered the heart of man, all that God has prepared for those who love Him. For to me God revealed them through the Spirit, for the Spirit searches all things, even the depths of God. For who among men knows the thoughts of a man but the spirit of the man within him? Even so, the thoughts of God no one knows but the Spirit of God. Now I have received, not the spirit of the world, but the Spirit who is from God, that I might know the things freely given to me by God.

I ask for wisdom and it is given to me generously. For nothing is hidden, except to be revealed; nor has anything been secret, but that it should come to light. He gives me wisdom and utterance, which none of my opponents can resist or refute.

Prosperity[2]

My God supplies all my needs according to His rich abundance of glory in Christ Jesus. He commands the blessing upon me in all that I put my hand to, and blesses me in the land He has given to me. All these blessings will come upon me and overtake me because I obey the voice of the Lord.

For when He made the promise to me, since He could swear by no one greater, He swore by Himself, saying, "I will surely bless you, and I will surely multiply you."

---

[2] *Adapted from Philippians 4:19; Deuteronomy 8:18; 28:2,8; Hebrews 6:13,14; Proverbs 10:22; Psalm 35:27; 37:4; 84:11; Malachi 3:10,11; 1 Timothy 6:17; 2 Corinthians 9:8.*

He has given me the power to make wealth, that He may confirm His covenant to me. His blessing makes me rich and He adds no sorrow to it. He delights in the prosperity of His servant.

I bring the tithe into the storehouse, so there may be food in His house, and I test Him in this, to see if He will not open for me the windows of heaven and pour out such blessing that there will not be room enough to receive it. He will rebuke the devourer for my sake.

He richly supplies me with all things to enjoy. I delight myself in Him and He gives me the desires of my heart. No good thing will He withhold from those who walk uprightly. He makes all grace abound to me. I always have everything I need, and I have an abundance for every good deed.

Favor[3]

He blesses the righteous and surrounds me with favor like a shield. The Lord is with me. He extends kindness to me and gives me favor. I keep increasing in wisdom and stature, and in favor with God and man.

His favor is for a lifetime; by it I am exalted. A good man will obtain favor from the Lord. I am greatly blessed and highly favored of the Lord.

I do not let kindness and truth leave me; I bind them around my neck, and I write them on the tablet of my heart. So I will find favor and good repute in the eyes of God and man.

Health[4]

I give attention to His words; I incline my ear to His sayings. I do not let them depart from my sight; I keep them in

---

[3] *Adapted from Psalm 5:12; 30:5; Ezra 7:28; Luke 1:28; 2:52; Proverbs 3:3,4; 12:2.*
[4] *Adapted from Proverbs 3:5-8; 4:20-22; Psalm 103:2-4, 107:20; Isaiah 53:4,5.*

the midst of my heart. For they are life to those who find them, and health to my whole body.

Bless the Lord, O my soul, and forget none of His benefits; who pardons all my iniquities, who heals all my diseases, and who redeems my life from the pit. He sent His Word and healed me.

I trust in the Lord with all my heart, and I do not lean on my own understanding. In all my ways I acknowledge Him, and He will make my paths straight. I am not wise in my own eyes; I fear the Lord and turn away from evil. It will be healing to my body, and health to my bones.

Surely my griefs He Himself bore, and my sorrows He carried. He was pierced through for my transgressions, He was crushed for my iniquities; the chastening for my well-being fell upon Him, and by His scourging I am healed.

Joy[5]

The joy of the Lord is my strength. He satisfies me in the morning with lovingkindness, that I might sing for joy and be glad all my days. This is the day which the Lord has made; I rejoice and I am glad in it. I shout with joy in the morning. A joyful heart has a continual feast.

I rejoice in His strength. How great is His joy in the victories He gives! He has granted me the desire of my heart and has not withheld the request of my lips. He placed a crown of pure gold on my head. He has given me life and length of days. He has granted me eternal blessings and made me glad with the joy of His presence.

I am continually filled with joy and with the Holy Spirit.

---

[5] *Adapted from Nehemiah 8:10; Psalm 21:1-6; 30:5,11; 36:8; 63:7; 90:14; 118:24; Proverbs 15:15; Acts 13:52; Romans 14:17; 15:13.*

The God of hope fills me with all joy and peace in believing. For His kingdom is righteousness, peace, and joy in the Holy Spirit. In the shadow of His wings, I sing for joy. I feast on the abundance of His house, and I drink from His river of delights. He has turned my mourning into dancing and clothed me with joy.

Love[6]

The love of God has been poured out in my heart through the Holy Spirit who was given to me. Therefore, I keep myself in the love of God, and all I do is done in love.

I am an imitator of God, and I walk in love, just as Christ also loved me. Above all, I keep fervent in my love for others, because love covers a multitude of sins. In obedience to the truth, I purify my soul for a sincere love of the brethren, and I fervently love others from the heart.

Love is patient, love is kind, and is not jealous; love does not brag and is not arrogant, does not act unbecomingly; it does not seek its own, is not provoked, does not take into account a wrong suffered, does not rejoice in unrighteousness, but rejoices with the truth; love bears all things, believes all things, hopes all things, endures all things. Love never fails.

Victory[7]

Whatever is born of God overcomes the world; and this is the victory that has overcome the world—my faith. I am born of God, and I overcome the world.

Thanks be to God, who always leads me in His triumph in Christ, and manifests through me the sweet aroma of the knowledge of Him in every place I go.

---

[6] *Adapted from Romans 5:5; Jude 21; 1 Corinthians 13:4-8; 16:14; Ephesians 5:1,2; 1 Peter 1:22; 4:8.*
[7] *Adapted from 1 John 4:4; 5:4; 2 Corinthians 2:14; Philippians 4:13; Romans 8:37.*

I can do all things through Him who makes me strong. In all things I overwhelmingly conquer through Him who loved me. I am from God and have overcome them, because greater is He who is in me than he who is in the world.

Blessing[8]

I am blessed with every spiritual blessing in the heavenly places in Christ. All these blessings come upon me and over-take me. I am blessed in the city, and blessed in the country. I am blessed when I come in, and blessed when I go out. I am blessed in my offspring. I abound in blessings. All the work of my hands is blessed. I am the head and not the tail, and I am above and not underneath.

Every good thing and every perfect gift is coming to me from the Father of lights. I am not afraid, for my Father has chosen gladly to give me the kingdom. Surely goodness and lovingkindness will follow me all the days of my life, and I will dwell in the house of the Lord forever.

The Lord blesses me, and keeps me; the Lord makes His face shine on me, and He is gracious to me. The Lord lifts up His countenance on me, and gives me peace.

I belong to Christ and I am Abraham's offspring, an heir according to promise. I am blessed with the blessings of Abraham.

Meditation[9]

This book of the law shall not depart from my mouth, but I shall meditate on it day and night, so that I might be careful

---

[8] *Adapted from Ephesians 1:3; Deuteronomy 28:2-13; James 1:17; Luke 12:32; Psalm 23:6; Numbers 6:24-26; Galatians 3:9,29.*

[9] *Adapted from Joshua 1:8; Hebrews 3:1; 4:14; 10:23; Deuteronomy 30:11,14; Psalm 1:1-3; James 1:25; Mark 11:22,23.*

to do according to all that is written in it; for then I will make my way prosperous, and then I will have success.

Because I have a great High Priest who has passed through the heavens, Jesus the Son of God, I hold fast the confession of my faith without wavering. Jesus is the Apostle and High Priest of my confession. His commandment is not too difficult for me, nor is it out of reach. But the Word is very near me, in my mouth and in my heart, that I should observe it.

How blessed is the man who does not walk in the counsel of the wicked, nor stand in the path of sinners, nor sit in the seat of scoffers. But my delight is in the law of the Lord, and in His law I meditate both day and night. I will be like a tree firmly planted by streams of water, which yields its fruit in its season, and its leaf does not wither, and whatever I do, prospers.

I look intently at the perfect law, the law of liberty, and I abide by it, not having become a forgetful hearer but an effectual doer. I am blessed in what I do.

I have faith in God. I speak to mountains and I do not doubt in my heart, but believe that what I say is going to happen, and it shall be.

Faith[10]

I respect the promises of God, and I do not waver in unbelief. I am strong in faith. I give glory to God. I am fully assured that what He promised, He is able to perform. All things are possible to me because I believe. It is done to me according to my faith.

The righteous shall live by faith. I have faith the size of a mustard seed and nothing is impossible to me. I fight the

[10] *Adapted from Romans 1:17; 4:20,21; Mark 9:23; Matthew 9:29; 17:20; 1 Timothy 6:12.*

good fight of faith; I take hold of eternal life; I make the good confession.

God's Word[11]

I bind His Word on my heart; I tie it around my neck. When I walk about, it will guide me; when I sleep, it will watch over me; when I awake, it will speak to me. I delight to do His will; His Word is within my heart. For He made this covenant with me, He put His Word upon my heart and wrote it upon my mind.

His Word is settled forever in heaven. He has magnified His Word according to His name. The sum of His Word is truth, and every one of His righteous ordinances is everlasting.

Prayer[12]

All things for which I pray and ask, I believe I have received them, and they are granted to me. I abide in Him, and His Word abides in me; I ask whatever I wish, and it is done for me.

Whatever I ask in His name, He will do, that the Father may be glorified in the Son. If I ask Him for anything in His name, He will do it. And everything I ask in prayer, believing, I shall receive.

If I ask the Father for anything, He will give it to me in Jesus' name. I ask and I receive, that my joy may be made full. This is the confidence I have before Him, that if I ask anything according to His will, He hears me. And if I know that He hears me in whatever I ask, I know that I have the requests which I have asked from Him.

[11] *Adapted from Proverbs 6:21,22; Psalm 40:8; 119:89,160; 138:2; Hebrews 10:16.*
[12] *Adapted from Mark 11:24; John 14:13,14; 15:7; 16:23,24; Matthew 21:22; 1 John 5:14,15.*

What's Next?

In *Book One*, we have covered some of the basic questions about faith. We first talked about building foundations that will last. Then we examined the importance of faith—why we need it. After that, we explored what faith is and how it grows. And finally, we looked at three examples of faith in action.

In *Book Two*, we will continue to discover more important truth concerning the topic of faith. First, we will take an in-depth look at the relationship between faith and God's Word. Then we will explore two important but controversial topics: healing and prosperity. We will conclude with an examination of the fight of faith. Two appendixes will be included—one will chronicle the lives of heroes of the faith throughout Church history, and the other will list all the healings found in the Gospels.

The life of faith is an exciting journey. I hope these books will provide a road map to help you navigate the many challenges along the way.

Paul Barker